The Power of Miracles

STORIES OF GOD
IN THE EVERYDAY

The Power of Miracles

STORIES OF GOD
IN THE EVERYDAY

Joan Wester Anderson

BALLANTINE BOOKS • NEW YORK

A Ballantine Book
Published by The Ballantine Publishing Group

Copyright © 1998 by Joan Wester Anderson

http://www.randomhouse.com

Library of Congress Cataloging-in-Publication Data
Anderson, Joan Wester.
The power of miracles : stories of god in the everyday /
Joan Wester Anderson. — 1st ed.
p.   cm.
Includes bibliographical references.
ISBN 0-345-39732-0 (alk. paper)
1. Miracles.   I. Title.
BT97.2.A5   1998
231.7'3—DC21   98-13966
CIP

Text design by Holly Johnson

Manufactured in the United States of America

First Edition: November 1998

10   9   8   7   6   5   4   3   2   1

To Elizabeth Zack, my editor at Ballantine, wise and professional beyond her years: Your light heart, tact, and encouragement are largely responsible for the publication of this book. Bless you.

Contents

CONTENTS

Acknowledgments

I would like to thank those who offered help and information in my writing efforts. They include those readers and friends who sent me story leads or were able to add details to pieces already written, including Celeste Shaw Sullivan of Arlington Heights, Illinois; Ethel Lynch Caldwell of Chicago, Illinois; Jacqueline Spierenburg of Bradenton, Florida; Jim Bramlett of Orlando, Florida; Barbara Gove of Horse Shoe, North Carolina; author Michael Brown of Latham, New York, and the gracious staffs at *Guideposts* magazine, New York, New York; BreakThrough Ministries, Lincoln, Virginia; and Media Fellowship International, in Kenmore, Washington.

A special word of appreciation to Mother Angelica of the Eternal Word Television Network and Father J. Michael Sparough, S. J., of the Jesuit Retreat League of Chicago, both of whom took time to instruct me on matters involving doctrine and Bible history, as well as Leonard LeSourd of Break-

Through who, before his 1996 death, provided some useful insights on heaven.

I'm grateful for the technical and professional assistance furnished by Julie Fitts Ritter of the Padre Pio Foundation of America; Michele Wolford, segment producer of the television series *Could It Be a Miracle?*; personnel at the *Fayetteville Observer-Times* (North Carolina); the television series *Unsolved Mysteries*; the Vineyard Christian Fellowship, Anaheim, California; National Opinion Research Center, University of Chicago; the Centers for Disease Control and Prevention, Atlanta, Georgia; and the Illinois State Police.

My thanks to film producers Albert Nader (Questar, Inc.), Peter Shockey (Cascom International, Inc.) and Linda and Chris Lewis (Entertainment Group), whose videos have supported my own efforts in researching angels, miracles, and prayers, as well as the radio and television talk show hosts from around the country who continue to air discussions on these subjects.

And, as always, special thanks go to my readers. You will never know how your constant support and willingness to share your stories with me and with one another enriches my own work. You have been, and continue to be, a joyous gift.

Signs from God

*I'm thankful, Lord, that all the
darkness in the world has never put
out Thy light.*

—UNKNOWN

I was about eight when I first became aware of
what a miracle was. In this case it involved
Jesus' mother, Mary. Even though she had died
a long time ago and had presumably gone to
heaven, as all good people do, she had also
somehow appeared to children about my age in
a place across the ocean called Fátima, Portugal,
to give them some messages. The apparitions

occurred in 1917, when our country was involved in the First World War (although we American Catholics did not hear about the sightings until decades later). Mary had told the children that everyone must pray for peace. If people did not, this current war would end but another more serious one would break out, and Russia would "spread its errors" throughout the world. The messages seemed incomprehensible to world leaders and were almost universally ignored. Yet just a few months after the apparitions ended, Communism took hold, and, a quarter century later, the Second World War did turn out to be worse than the First.

Although the political significance was beyond my young grasp, I was fascinated with the idea that heaven and earth could intersect in this way; that Mary (or as we called her, the Blessed Mother) could visit earth for a particular purpose.

As I grew, I heard of other visions, some involving just Mary, others with her and Jesus. All offered similar messages: *God loves you. Ask for forgiveness. Amend your lives. Pray for peace.* But the Catholic Church is slow to investigate and accept such events as genuine (although Fátima was eventually authenticated), and news of amazing happenings in other Christian denominations were rare and were usually "over there," halfway around the world in some remote area, having little influence on my daily life. Miracles, I eventually decided, were spectacular sun-spinning events, bestowed on rare occasions upon *special* saints, so the rest of us would not forget our ultimate destiny: heaven.

In the mid-1980s, however, my thinking changed. Because our family received a miracle of its own.

"THE NEW AGE OF ANGELS—WHAT IN HEAVEN IS GOING ON?"—*Time* magazine, December 27, 1993

I've written about it before—how our son was rescued from freezing to death on the side of a road. By—there couldn't be any question about it—an angel disguised as a tow truck driver, who mysteriously disappeared. The event sent me on another quest about miracles, with new queries. If God would do this for us, just an ordinary family, would He, was He doing this for others? Yes! It seemed to be a well-kept secret, but soon I found more than enough people from a wide variety of religious faiths with angel stories to contribute to a book. It was titled *Where Angels Walk,* and I doubted many would read it. Yet, less than two years later, the popularity of angels had swept the country so incredibly that talk shows featured them, stores carrying nothing but angel merchandise opened, and both *Time* and *Newsweek* devoted their Christmas covers to the subject. What was happening—just a new trend? In part. But as *Time* noted, "If heaven is willing to sing to us, it is little to ask that we be willing to listen."

As angels remained popular, I noticed something else: an increase in the amount and intensity of mystical occurrences being reported among "ordinary people." Now that the floodgates had opened, people no longer hesitated to stand up at a conference or in a church audience and give testimony to a wonderful event in their own lives. As a nation, we were becoming more comfortable relating earth to heaven. Instead of miracles being uncommon and limited to saintly figures, it seemed that many of us were—and are—touching a piece of God's glory.

And accounts of miracles keep increasing. People bearing the stigmata (the five wounds of Christ) are being revealed in both the United States and other countries. There are numerous reported visions of the Mother of Jesus. Although Medjugorje in the former Yugoslavia is her most long-running alleged appearance (daily since 1981), she is no longer limited to hillsides in predominantly Catholic areas but seems to be touching all cultures, appearing on a Coptic Orthodox church in Zeitoun, Egypt; in Rwanda (never asking that the Protestant and Muslim people of Africa convert to Catholicism but calling everyone her own "dear children"); in Damascus and Korea. Since April 1987, on the first anniversary of the explosion in Chernobyl, as many as half a million people have claimed to see ongoing apparitions of her, accompanied by angels, in the Ukraine.

Nor are such messages limited to the Mother of Christ. Protestant missionaries too are recounting an amazing flow of God's spirit in places such as Australia, Taiwan, Thailand, and the Philippines. For example, ". . . a great miraculous outpouring of our time . . . erupted in 1971 at a Bible school in Nha Trang, South Vietnam, during the dark days of the Vietnam War," writes Paul Prather in *Modern Day Miracles*. "Spontaneously, students began to confess their sins and to minister to each other with a tremendous sense of joy. They decided to go out witnessing about their newly charged faith. Wherever they went, miracles shot out from the Nha Trang Biblical and Theological Institute into the countryside like Roman candles. Sensational healings and exorcisms became particularly common, but there were also reports of dead bodies that resurrected through prayer." Missionaries continue to report similar amazing happenings.

"Spiritual signals" are also happening within religions other than Christianity. In the mid-90s, there were four lunar eclipses over Jerusalem, all coinciding with significant Jewish holy days; in 1994, the birth of an all-white buffalo in Janesville, Wisconsin, fulfilled a Native American legend that portends new spiritual knowledge.

About that same time, reports came from India that statues of Ganesha, the Hindu deity with the head of an elephant, had started drinking milk from spoons. Word quickly spread across the world, via phone calls and CNN coverage to temples in the United States and elsewhere, cutting across caste and education, as Hindus by the millions flocked to their holy places with milk. Ultimately most Indian scientists debunked it as a fraud. Yet it undoubtedly drew the Hindu world's attention to spiritual matters—just as tears flowing from Greek Orthodox icons, the sun spinning at holy shrines, and other unexplainable happenings seem to do for other groups.

"Some people argue that supernatural acts reported by religions other than their own are superstitions, the results of hysteria or even hoaxes," Prather writes. "Still others hold that God is quite willing to perform miracles for people who happen not to belong to their own organization. . . ." The Roman Catholic Church's most recent catechism states specifically that God doesn't necessarily limit his work to Christians,

much less to members of particular denominations. Everyone that He has created is His child
and is loved equally.

But God has *always* loved His children. So
why does He seem to be sending more miracles
today than ever before? "There has never been a
global outpouring of divine manifestations of
this magnitude in the known history of the
world," writes Janice T. Connell in *Meetings with
Mary*. "[The] visionaries of Medjugorje have said
that no one in the world will be excluded from
the messages delivered by the Blessed Mother.
People everywhere are becoming aware of the
seriousness of the times and the opportunities
entrusted to humanity." Even if some of these
manifestations, such as the Hindu milk episode,
are hard to interpret or fraudulent or very private and personal, the sheer number encourages
us to believe that God is sending signals to His
people, especially now as the millennium ap-
proaches. He wants our love and attention
because, without Him, life is so much more difficult to understand and endure. He wants to be
first in our hearts.

In many cases, however, heaven is meeting

resistance. "For our battle is not against human forces but against the principalities and powers, the rulers of this world of darkness, the evil spirits in regions above" (Ephesians 6:12). According to the Bible, there have always been satanic beings roaming the earth, tempting humans to turn their backs on God and live lives of selfishness and sin. And this perceived recent increase in heavenly activity has no doubt generated the same level of intensity on "the other side," leading to what some call "spiritual warfare," the ultimate battle for souls.

"WHAT'S AHEAD FOR AMERICA? CHRISTIAN LEADERS SHARE THEIR CONCERNS ABOUT THE SPIRITUAL STATE OF THE UNION."—*Charisma*, October 1996

"Last year Americans spent more than $8 billion on hard-core videos, peep shows, . . . adult cable programming . . . computer porn and sex magazines—an amount much larger than Hollywood's domestic box office receipts and larger than all the revenues generated by rock and country music recordings."—*US News & World Report*, February 10, 1997

"SIGNS AND WARNINGS: HAS THE FINAL HOUR BEGUN?"—Signs of the Times, January, February, March, 1994

It doesn't take an expert to note that, despite God's attempts to reach us, there is still a lot of chaos and suffering in our world. Children weep over a broken home; teenagers find life deprived of meaning; young couples worry about finances and broken promises; the elderly grapple with disease and loneliness; and there are wars, famine, prejudice, destruction of nature . . . the list goes on. If God truly loves us, why does He allow all this to happen?

- *Sometimes hard times occur through no fault of our own, but are just a result of living in an imperfect world.* God does not send suffering to his children, but, as C. S. Lewis once noted, "Pain is God's megaphone:" It gets our attention. When these periods come, our job is to simply endure, getting through them with the help of God and those around us. Perhaps the struggle will teach us lessons that we can use later, to help others.

- *People who are attempting to move closer to God will often find obstacles in their paths.* There is a saying that "if you're not doing anything for the Kingdom, Satan leaves you alone. But if you're becoming an effective soldier, you'll find yourself under attack." Members of my Wednesday-night prayer group often joke that if the weather is going to be bad, the car breaks down, or a headache is going to develop, it will happen on a Wednesday, giving us an excuse to stay away from our two-hour prayer time and the graces and spiritual insights that might have resulted. But the Bible confirms our observation: "My child," says the Book of Sirach, 2:1, "when you come to serve the Lord, expect trouble." The solution here is to persevere. Relief will come.

- *Suffering happens too, as a result of sin, freely*

chosen. Should we be surprised when children, raised on a steady diet of gross and immoral movies and television programs, act out what they see? Should we be surprised when people then dabble in the occult, settle problems through violence or abandon their responsibilities? One emergency room physician, whose name I can't recall, told me his personal theory: that if people simply lived by the Ten Commandments, we would have no health care crisis in our country, because hospitals would not need to treat gunshot wounds, victims of spousal or child abuse, and those suffering from sexually transmitted diseases or drug overdoses (the list could go on and on). Instead, hospitals could use their resources for those ill from disease.

As God continues to try to get our attention, what lies ahead? Few people believe that the current era heralds the end of the world or the Second Coming; Jesus told us no one knew the day or the hour that would occur. But will there be a repeat of what happened when the Fátima prophecies of 1917 went unheeded? Or are we heading toward some sort of world-wide "moment of truth" or chastisement, where God's people may have to summon the courage to take a stand or get involved in society as never before?

Perhaps. But it's possible that there may be more wondrous events ahead too. One pastor had a vision in which he saw himself in a crowded football stadium. Suddenly the Holy Spirit was beside each person in the stadium. Instantly everything stopped, for God was showing every man, woman, and child just where he or she stood on the pathway of life and eternity, in his or her relationship to God and to evil. People began to weep, just to see the glory of heaven revealed in that way—and to realize how they measured up against what they had been given.

Whatever comes, we know that God will make *all* things—even the hardest situations—work for the good of those who love Him.

What an awesome time to be alive and to see how God can turn difficulties into shining moments of hope and glory!

So this is a mystery book, one without an ending. It includes people (*denotes a name change) not only from the United States but from other countries, who have been touched easily and beautifully by the hand of God or one of God's angels. And it also includes those who have gone through Job-like experience of a suffering or difficulty that challenged many of their beliefs. Yet they hung on and can testify that, despite whatever we may witness in the coming years, God will keep His promise:

"If my people . . . humble themselves and pray, and seek my presence and turn from their wicked ways, I will hear them from heaven, and pardon their sins and heal their land" (2 Chronicles 7:14).

Not my Way but Yours . . .

You are to be my witnesses . . .
even to the ends of the earth.

—*ACTS 1:8*

When Duane Miller awakened on Sunday morning, January 14, 1990, his throat was raw, his voice a bit raspy. But he barely gave it a thought. Scheduled to preach two morning services that day, he was already mentally reviewing his material: Would his congregation be consoled, informed, hopefully inspired by his words? As senior pastor of First Baptist Church in Brenham, Texas, Duane loved God, loved to preach and sing (he had started singing professionally at the age of sixteen), and loved family life with his wife, Joylene, and their two college-age daughters. And although his church was suffering through some financial problems—which often resulted in twenty-hour workdays for Duane—his natural optimism was strong. With God on his side, what could go wrong?

Now, however, as Duane prepared for the day, he experienced that ominous stuffy, head-achy, dizzy feeling that usually heralds the flu. Drinking hot tea, he managed to preach at the first service, but singing was all but impossible—even his range seemed limited to just a few notes. "During my second sermon, every sound and inflection grated on the back of my throat like sandpaper," Duane recalls. He cut his talk short, canceled the rest of his duties, and reluctantly went home to bed. Obviously the long work hours had finally caught up with him.

The flu took almost ten days to abate. But Duane's throat did not recover. "It was painful and constricted, as if someone had my windpipe between his two fingers and was squeezing it whenever I swallowed," he explains. "There was a constant choking sensation. My voice was weak and hoarse." When Duane finally saw a physician, the throat was so swollen that the doctor could not get a scope down to examine it. Duane's nightmare had begun.

The doctor was almost certain of the diagnosis: He suspected that the flu germ had penetrated the protective sheath around the vocal cords and permanently destroyed them. Duane was probably going to live the rest of his life without a normal voice. But there was the possibility that the doctor's suspicions weren't correct. He wanted Duane to try some medication and visit several specialists.

When, fourteen days later, there seemed to be no real improvement from the medication he had started taking, Duane went to the Baylor College of Medicine in Houston for more tests. On their recommendation, he took a six-month leave of absence from his church, in order to stay home and speak as infrequently as possible. Perhaps his voice—his whole body—was just worn out and needed some time to recover.

Duane was discouraged during this time, but

not panic-stricken. After all, he was a man of faith, who believed that God could and often did heal. God was obviously taking His time about answering Duane's prayers, but of course He *would* answer. Hadn't He called Duane to the ministry, where speaking was absolutely essential? Despite his fears, Duane was willing to wait until God disclosed more of His always-perfect plan.

But God revealed nothing and as time passed new symptoms developed: Duane lost his equilibrium, and often his vision would blur. Was he going to lose his sight now as well as his voice? Life slowly became unworkable, unbearable. How could one communicate, earn, even take care of errands without being able to make the most minimal of sounds? Financial difficulties grew. "The mortgage company, phone company, the grocer—no one gives discounts just because you've lost your voice," Duane says. But surely the answers would come.

They did not. After the leave of absence ended, Duane's voice hadn't improved, and the physicians offered no new alternatives. The original diagnosis had been correct: There was no hope of reversing this situation. Duane could still emit some sounds, but these were produced by fatty tissue near the vocal cords (known as "false cords"), and in time these too would wear away. Within a year or so, the doctors agreed, Duane would be completely mute.

Brokenhearted, Duane officially resigned his pastorate. The family returned to First Baptist Church in Houston, one of the largest church communities in the country, where Duane had served for twelve years prior to going to Brenham, and where they had many old friends. "I faced the indignity of more medical tests, the humiliation of being without a vocational future, the anguish of watching my singing and preaching ministry being completely shut down," Duane writes in his book, *Out of the Silence*. "But I no longer faced them alone." Duane had always been the giver in this congregation; now he was in need. It was not the role he would have chosen, but for a little while, being surrounded by friends made life more bearable.

Joylene and the girls found jobs (which paid the college bills), Duane ran an agency involving work he could do on paper rather than vocally, and the family managed to rent a house they all liked very much. And when several physicians were almost positive that Duane had multiple sclerosis, the final test result was negative. In the midst of the agony, there was always just a trace of hope.

Duane was fully aware that people suffered handicaps and physical pain far more crippling than his. And yet, his voice was essential to the job he had always *assumed* God had called him to do. What had changed? Did God now find him unworthy? "The anguish of my physical impairment began to bludgeon my spiritual life as well," Duane recalls. "If I hear anyone who goes through a trying test say he or she never doubted God, I think that person is either lying or has lost touch with reality." *What are you doing, God? Don't You love me anymore? Have You abandoned me?* How many people throughout history, both famous and obscure, have struggled with these questions? Duane Miller was no exception.

By now, because his condition was so rare, Duane had become a medical celebrity. At one seminar in Switzerland, specialists from all over the world examined photos of his throat. "From the very beginning, everything had been recorded and documented, like time-lapse photography," he explains, "because every time I went to see any doctor, he would put the scope down my throat and photograph the changes, especially the growing scar tissue."

It was as if God wanted everything officially recorded—wanted everyone to see that the glory, when it came, would be all His.

During the past agonizing years, Duane had learned to make himself heard by using a sort of guttural pressure, forcing air through his throat and "screaming" at the top of his lungs. Finally someone from the congregation found a microphone that, when pressed against Duane's lips, could amplify these sounds, which opened up a new possibility: Perhaps Duane could occasionally teach his former Sunday school class at First Baptist. He was hesitant. Who would want to listen to such uncomfortable sounds? But his friends encouraged him, and once in a while he preached a short lesson.

He was doing just that on the morning of January 17, 1993, having been persuaded into substituting at the last minute for another teacher. The class was also being tape-recorded, a routine practice. The two hundred or so attendees knew about Duane's voice. But because Duane had always tried to keep the more personal problems to himself, no one in the audience was aware that he had recently lost his job and his medical insurance, had had a book proposal rejected (not because of his writing ability but because he would not be physically able to do any media promotion), or that he was nearing the time when the doctors believed he would become completely mute—in short, that he was as low as he had been since the beginning of his ordeal. Nor had Duane selected that particular day's lesson, based on Psalm 103, since the series was scheduled seven years in advance. "I was feeling no great faith—in fact, inside, I was still asking God, *Why have You punished me this way?*" Duane recalls.

In Psalm 103, God reminds us not to forget:

Who forgives all your sins,
Who heals all your diseases,
Who redeems your life from the pit . . .

So that your youth is renewed like the
    eagle's.

These were hard concepts for Duane to dis-
cuss. He truly believed that God does such
things. But everyone in the congregation had
watched Duane struggle for three years; they
knew that God had not healed or renewed their
beloved friend, despite his courage and goodness. How effective a teaching could this be?

Duane spoke for more than twenty minutes
before reaching these particular verses, and he
was just about ready to cut the lesson short—his
throat was hurting terribly. The strain of pushing
the words out was so great that he wondered if
anyone could hear him anyway. "I have had,
and you've had, pit experiences," he forged on.
Pit experiences . . . That's where he was now, in a
pit with no way out. . . . Suddenly, on the word
pit, Duane felt something odd. The "hands" that
had been locking his throat for three years
seemed to let go! People looked up—what had
happened? Duane sounded different.

Duane noticed it too. His voice was
stronger, less hoarse. "Now . . . to say God

doesn't do miracles today is to put God in a box, and God doesn't like to be put in a box," he said. Then he stopped, stunned. He could hear himself! His voice was normal!

Joylene left her chair in the audience and ran up to the stage. "I don't . . . understand this right now," Duane said without the microphone. "In fact, I'm at a loss for words!" He put his arms around Joylene and began to weep. Some in the congregation broke into tears; some cheered, laughed, and praised God.

Others dashed out of the room to find the senior pastor. "Duane's been healed!" they shouted.

Could it be true? "I wanted to laugh, cry, sing, shout, dance, and hug everyone I could, all at the same time," Duane recalls. "After a few brief minutes, I thought, *What better way to celebrate the restoration of my voice than to teach God's word?*" So he continued the lesson. And at the end of the session, the congregation burst into the most appropriate of all endings, the doxology: Praise God from Whom all blessings flow. . . . "I don't think anyone who was there that day will ever sing the doxology in a casual manner again," Duane says. "The truth of its simplicity struck our hearts for eternity."

Word, of course, had started to spread. Dr. John Bisagno, senior pastor of the church, was conducting the scheduled worship service in the main church and now summoned Duane to the platform. People who had attended the early service had heard about Duane's restored voice, so now there was standing room only in the worship center as Dr. Bisagno approached the pulpit.

"You all know Duane Miller," Dr. Bisagno began. "He's been around here for the best part of twenty years. And most of you know the problem he has had with his voice these past three years. I want him to come and tell you what God has done in his life."

Duane approached the pulpit. "Well, I'll try," he said. At that, some five thousand people jumped to their feet and began to worship God much as Duane's earlier class had done. Some wept, some laughed, others clapped; many fell to their knees and their tears flowed freely. The organist began to play the Bill Gaither chorus, "Let's Just Praise the Lord!" And everyone did.

Since his healing, Duane has been back to many physicians for reevaluation, and every photo taken of his throat since January 17, 1993, shows a complete lack of scar tissue on his vocal cords. They are as smooth and as healthy as they were before his tribulation began, with absolutely no indication that any problem ever existed. "Even if you could explain the coincidence of me suddenly being able to speak," Duane says, "you have to understand that scar tissue doesn't disappear by itself. What happened to it?"

And yet, after much thought, Duane is convinced that this is the central message of his entire experience. Scar tissue—at least the spiritual kind—*does* disappear. God has said that He will perform glorious works for His children, and what could be more glorious than knowing that our lives, with all their failures and mistakes, can be completely restored in an instant, through His love and grace?

Nor should the very *public* aspect of Duane's miracle be overlooked. Not only did the witnesses in his congregation and throughout Houston experience a deepening of their faith, but word spread throughout the world, primarily because the entire event had been tape-recorded. So often miracles are private, tender in their intimacy. But in this case, God had unleashed the tongues of thousands, all eager to share this good news. Ironically, Duane himself is one of them, now a radio talk show host each day on KKHT in Houston—when he's not on the road preaching what he believes to be an important lesson to audiences in every part of the country. "God healed me, not because I earned it, deserved it, had enough people praying, or any of those other reasons," Duane says, "but because He wanted people to be drawn to Him and to give Him all the glory."

Many believe that this is just the beginning of the glory God is going to reveal to His people in the coming years. Our God—yours, mine, and Duane's—is truly an awesome God.[1]

What God Has Done

Will doctors soon tell us, "Say two prayers and call me in the morning?"

—*(AP) DECEMBER 6, 1995*

Duane Miller was healed of a physical condition. But that's not the only way God is healing today.

For example, an "angel" who let me know about a very special healing is Jim McNamara of Mokena, Illinois. Jim worked for Sears Roebuck in the Chicago area, and his job involved calling on people in their homes. "I had found the Lord, in a big way," Jim says, "so from time to time, I'd witness about Him to customers if they seemed open to it."

One day Jim had an appointment with an older couple, Mr. and Mrs. Sam Lynch, who lived on Chicago's South Side. Their warmth and hospitality were evident, and Jim liked them immediately. "After we concluded our business," Jim recalls, "I noticed a huge Bible lying on their coffee table. 'That's a very important book, isn't it?' I asked the couple."

They both nodded. "It certainly is."

Briefly, Jim told them about how he had come to know Jesus. When he had finished, Louise Lynch nodded to her husband. "Tell him what happened to you, Sam," she said.

"Well," Sam said shyly, "I'm a carpenter. And one day I felt the Lord asking me to build a church for him. And so I did."

"You did? A whole church?" Jim was astounded.

"Well, I subcontracted some of the work. But I did the plans, and most of the labor. It's still open today. The Leclaire Missionary Baptist Church, on Lavergne Avenue. My name is even in a piece of the concrete wall." Sam sat back.

But there was more to the story. "Tell him what happened after it was built," Louise prodded.

Sam squirmed in his chair. Apparently, this part was harder to relate. "When they were making plans to dedicate the church, the deacons and people wanted me to read the Bible from the pulpit," Sam explained. "I kept saying no, but they kept asking."

"Why didn't you want to read?" Jim asked.

The Lynches looked at each other. "He couldn't," Louise said softly. "Sam had been illiterate his whole life. In fact, my mother originally forbade me to marry him because he couldn't read. She didn't think he would amount to anything."

The couple eventually wed, but they had always kept Sam's disability a secret. No one had ever known about it except the three Lynch children who, as they grew, would read to their father from newspapers and books. Sam had a quick mind and a marvelous memory, so no one ever guessed his secret. But now, if people from the new congregation kept pressuring Sam, perhaps he would have to admit it. Neither he nor Louise was happy about that.

Eventually Louise came up with a solution. "We'll choose some verses," she told Sam. "And I'll read them over and over to you, and you'll memorize them. Then you can stand up at the pulpit, and it will *look* like you're reading. No one will ever know."

Sam relented. "We practiced pretty hard, every night," he told Jim. "But the verses were short, and no one knew what I was planning to read anyway, so I figured I could get through it."

The morning of the dedication came, and the church was full. Louise was sitting in the first row, and she watched proudly as Sam ascended the steps to the pulpit, picked up the open Bible, and began to read. And then . . . her heart seemed to stop.

For Sam was not reciting the verses they had practiced together. Nor was he repeating anything remotely resembling material he knew or was familiar with. No, instead he was *reading*— loudly, confidently, even turning pages.

Jim had listened to the story, enthralled. "How did the people in the audience react?" he now asked.

"They didn't know anything special was going on," Louise answered. "Since no specific material had been planned, they just assumed Sam was reading what he had selected. He went on and on. I don't think even he fully realized what was happening."

"I didn't," Sam added. "Not until I got home and the whole impossible situation hit me. Then I picked up a book—just to see if it had been some big mistake. And you know what? I could still read."

For the rest of his life Sam read, although sometimes a little slowly. Eventually he engaged a tutor who came to the house and helped him progress even more. But he and Louise never forgot the marvel of that special day in church.

"God healed the blind man," Jim McNamara says. "He said, 'Lazarus, come out!' And He must have said, 'Sam, read My Scriptures.' What a God we serve!"

———

A woman named Margaret approached my book-signing table with another example of healing. "I had gone to a big shopping mall for a job interview and left my two- and three-year-old girls with the baby-sitting service the stores provided," she explained. "Now the interview was over and I had picked up the girls. I stood at the top of the escalator in my suit and high heels, looking down three floors through all that chrome and glass and feeling a bit disoriented." With her left arm she was carrying her two-year-old, her purse, and a rather heavy diaper bag. With her right hand, Margaret was attempting to pull her three-year-old, Tammy, onto the escalator.

But Tammy was afraid to step on the moving stairs. "Mommy, I don't want to go!" she shrieked. Any moment Margaret was going to lose either her grip or her balance. "I was already a very nervous mother, someone who saw danger almost everywhere," Margaret admitted. "Right now I was working up to a panic. How were we going to get down safely?"

No one seemed to be near them, but then Margaret saw a firm hand come down on

Tammy's shoulder. The hand belonged to a dapper-looking elderly gentleman with white hair, wearing a dark suit. "He had smiling eyes," Margaret recalled. "Even though I was almost paranoid about strangers being near the girls, I felt comfortable with him right away."

The man eased Tammy onto the escalator and nodded at Margaret, as if to say, *I'm holding your little girl. She won't fall.*

Margaret nodded back, saying thank you without words.

The ride down was over in seconds, and during the brief flurry of getting her daughters off the escalator, Margaret lost sight of the elderly guardian. When she looked up, he had vanished—although he had been behind them and, to her recollection, hadn't stepped around them. There was no one matching his description anywhere around the sparsely populated mall, not even walking away from them. Where had the helpful stranger gone?

"Tammy," she asked, "did you see where that man went?"

Tammy looked up. "What man, Mommy?"

"The man on the escalator. The one who

put his hand on your shoulder so you wouldn't fall."

Tammy looked puzzled. "There wasn't any man on the escalator, Mommy. There was just us."

In a sudden burst of comprehension, Margaret saw. She had been given a glimpse of Tammy's guardian angel. And a message, too. For now, infused into her spirit were the words that seemed to accompany that long look she and the elderly man had exchanged. *As you see me now, with my hand on your child,* he had somehow told her, *I am,* always. *So there is no need to be so anxious. You cannot add one day to your child's life by worrying, nor take one away that is not already in God's plan.*

But what you can do, what you must *do, is love your children, with the kind of love only a mother can give, for however long they have been placed in your care. This is your most important job.*

"In an instant," Margaret told me, "I was healed of my fear, my constant worry over every aspect of my daughters' lives. And I remain so to this day. I'm concerned and watchful, but not panicky—and there's a big difference."

No ordinary encounter could have brought such a profound and instant emotional healing, Margaret said. She had been touched by a messenger of God.

Sister Maurella Schlise, a Catholic nun from Fargo, North Dakota, had served others in many ways, primarily as a teacher and a hospital chaplain. But never as a prison visitor, not until one Christmas when she traveled, as she usually did for the holidays, to the Florida home of her sister and brother-in-law, Rosemary and Pat Ryan. The Ryans had started a prison ministry, conducting weekly nondenominational prayer meetings at a nearby maximum-security penitentiary. Usually, no more than thirty-five men ever attended, but Rosemary and Pat refused to become discouraged. If, for just a little while, prayer lifted these prisoners out of despair and regret to focus on the One Who loved them despite it all, the hours Rosemary and Pat donated were well worth it.

Visitors were never allowed to bring anything to the prison, not even food. But when

Sister Maurella arrived at the Ryans' house, she found food preparations in full swing—not just for the family but for the prisoners, too. "Because our regular prayer meeting falls on Christmas Eve this year, the prison officials decided we could bring each of the men a few 'goodies,'" Rosemary explained to Sister Maurella. "We're going to make some Rice Krispies bars and homemade cookies for them. Enough to fill about fifty bags."

"Fifty bags! I thought you said the turnout was pretty low," Sister Maurella pointed out.

"It usually is. But maybe on Christmas Eve, some extra men will come. We wouldn't want to run out of food. Besides, for most of the inmates this will be their only gift."

Sister Maurella was glad she had arrived several days early to help with holiday preparations. Rosemary obviously had even more to do than usual.

The following morning Sister Maurella attended mass. She thought about the inmates, wondering if they—if anyone—could actually experience the miracle of Christmas from behind bars. What would it be like? Then, "Although

God is not in the habit of speaking directly to me," she says, smiling, "I distinctly heard a voice in my spirit. It specifically said, *Bring one hundred bags of candy and cookies to the prison.*

One hundred. It seemed far too many for this small group. "I thought it might be my imagination," Sister says. "But then I decided to step out in faith and tell Rosemary and Pat about it."

Rosemary and Pat were skeptical. But they too had had experiences when God seemed to "nudge" them just a little, and they respected Sister Maurella's insight. If Sister was wrong, the worst that could happen was that there would be some bags left over, and there were always plenty of places to donate extra sweets at Christmas.

The women spent Christmas Eve doing many chores, as well as filling one hundred white bags with homemade treats and candy. "The men will be pleased, I think," Rosemary mused. "Each will be happy to have a little gift all his own."

After dinner, they loaded the car and drove to the prison gates. The guards waved them through. Sister Maurella looked around. So this was what a penitentiary looked like. Now someone was hurrying toward them. "That's the chaplain," Rosemary explained.

"The chapel is filled!" the chaplain called. "I've never seen it so crowded. There must be a hundred men inside!"

A hundred! Rosemary and Sister Maurella smiled at each other. The little nudge from heaven had been real, after all. How glad they were that they had acted on it and prepared extra food.

Pat carried the box of white bags into the chapel, planning to begin the meeting in the usual way. But the prisoners had a surprise for them. They had prepared their own Christmas program. An inmate with a vibrant voice sang the moving story of the Little Drummer Boy. Another performed the Ave Maria, having somehow discovered that it was one of Rosemary's favorites. Everyone sang hymns, and one man read the Christmas story from the Bible. The chapel was hushed, small candles providing the only light. It was truly the most poignant Christmas Eve service that Sister Maurella had ever attended.

Finally the program ended, and the men eagerly lined up. Sister Maurella and Rosemary handed each one a white bag. "Thank you, Sister; thank you, Miz Ryan," they murmured . . . until ten men still stood in line. But the bags were gone. There had not been one hundred men in chapel. There had been one hundred and ten.

One hundred and ten! Sister Maurella was distraught. If God had truly spoken to her, why hadn't He told her to bring one hundred and ten bags? What should they do? *God, multiply the bags,* Rosemary prayed silently.

But a young convict had also seen their dilemma. "Sister," he spoke quietly, "we others . . . we'll share our bags with them."

Sister Maurella looked at the faces surrounding her. Men of every color and nationality; murderers, thieves . . . But men who now, because of His birthday, were willing to reach out to one another in forgiveness and love. Healing sometimes came in tiny steps, Sister knew. But once begun, it could grow.

The young convict opened his bag, preparing to divide his sweets. Just then, a prison trustee entered the chapel, carrying a sack. "Rosemary, we had some leftovers from a group that came this morning," he said. "Can you use them?"

Rosemary took the sack. Inside were candy and cookies—divided into ten white bags.

The group was astonished. "You see?" Rosemary smiled as she handed the bags to the remaining men. "Our God loves us so much that He cares for us in even the smallest ways."

Everyone rejoiced as the ten men received their treats. Especially Sister Maurella. She had wondered if Christmas could come in a prison, but now she knew. Where love is, God is.

Although born and raised Catholic, Mary Wayman had, for a variety of reasons, been away from her church for more than ten years. "I tried a few other denominations, but never got very comfortable with them and didn't join anywhere," she says. So she was a bit surprised when a longtime friend of hers who was a very active Catholic handed her a medal of the Virgin

Mary and Child. The friend explained that a woman in her church travels frequently to Medjugorje, the shrine in the former Yugoslavia, and takes various items there to be blessed by the Virgin. This was one of those blessed medals. Although Mary knew that the medal had no power on its own and is only a symbol of the Blessed Virgin and her concern for her children, she was touched that her friend had thought to give it to her, someone who didn't even go to a Catholic church. She started carrying the medal in her pocket every day.

Mary is a horsewoman and has owned several over the years. She had recently purchased a mare named Abby who was, she had decided, the best horse she had ever owned. "We just fit together—I loved her," she says. On a freezing Sunday afternoon a few weeks after receiving the medal, Mary drove to the stable where she boards Abby. "I walked out to the pasture and brought her into the barn to check on a problem she'd been having with her feet," Mary says. "She didn't act like herself at all; she wouldn't even take a treat from me, and all horses love treats. After watching her for a while, it was becoming obvious that she was in the beginning stages of colic."

The word *colic* strikes fear into the hearts of horse owners; the illness is probably the single biggest killer of horses. If a horse's colon becomes twisted, its blood supply is cut off and the colon dies from lack of circulation—and that means certain death for the horse. Mary called her veterinarian, who came immediately and indeed agreed that Abby's colon was not functioning as it should. He gave the mare some medication.

For the rest of the afternoon and into the evening, Mary and the barn owner kept Abby under surveillance, doing whatever they could to make her well. But by 10:00 P.M. they phoned the vet again. When he came by, the news was not good: Abby was worse than she had been on his first visit. The vet gave her another injection for the pain.

Just then Mary remembered the medal in her pocket. It had been there all along, but she hadn't thought to ask heaven for a healing for Abby. Did people do such things for animals? she wondered. Especially people like her—someone who hadn't been giving God a lot of attention lately? Was she worthy to pray?

But hadn't God said He would listen to anyone? Now Mary stood, holding the medal tightly, and pleaded for a miracle. "I then placed the medal on Abby's left side and prayed that her colon would resume functioning. I walked round to the other side and did the same thing." A few moments later Mary and the barn manager ran into the house to get warm, but while there, they again heard Abby thrashing. "We found her lying in her stall, convulsing with pain and unable to stand. We called the vet again."

Between the three of them, they managed to get Abby up and out of her stall. Her pulse rate had skyrocketed. Her gums were gray and there were no sounds of her colon functioning. "The vet looked at me with the saddest expression," Mary says. "We both knew that this beautiful mare wasn't going to make it. We tried to decide where to take her"—horses when euthanized must be brought to the spot where they are to be buried, if possible, because they are so large and heavy—"and finally decided on an area where the barn keeper's horse had been buried the previous spring."

So in minus-ten-degree weather, the barn keeper, the vet, and Mary slowly walked Abby to the place where she would receive her final injection.

Just as they were getting ready to do so, however, Abby's head shot up. She whinnied to the horses back in the barn and began rooting around in the snow for something to eat!

"Let me check her again," said the vet in disbelief. A moment later he was shaking his head. "Her pulse rate has dropped back to normal. I can hear sounds in her colon, too."

Mary was afraid to hope. Was it just a false alarm? But once they returned to the barn, the vet checked the horse's gums, only to find that they were now bright and pink!

Although Mary watched Abby all night long for signs of her illness returning, it never did. "I have absolutely no doubt that my prayers resulted in a miracle that saved Abby's life," Mary says. "She had been too far gone for any other explanation. Needless to say, my faith has been fully restored, and I'll never doubt in the power of prayer or God ever again. I wear the medal on a silver chain around my neck every day."

The visionaries at Medjugorje have been told that glories will be experienced all over the world, to people of all faiths, as a result of the Virgin Mary's appearances there. No one has specifically mentioned horses being healed.

But why not?

Nothing Is Impossible

My God, how wonderful thou art,
Thy majesty how bright!
—*F. W. FABER, ORATORY HYMNS*
"THE ETERNAL FATHER," 1854

God has also promised His people dominion over the earth itself, and the inanimate objects in it, as long as we respect it all. The great Episcopalian mystic Agnes Sanford, after asking God if it was permissible to pray for sunshine, would pray specifically to stop a storm, and dramatic things would often happen. However, most of us wouldn't even think about asking for such things. But Nel Van Schaik Roeleveld has tried it—and she believes.

Nel grew up in Nazi-occupied Holland, where life was extremely difficult. But her close-knit family always believed God was looking out for them. One evening, it was Nel's turn to set the table for dinner although, as she well knew, there was not a bit of food in the house. "What should I do, Daddy?" she asked.

"Set the table anyway, and we'll pray," was his reply.

As the family began the Our Father, they heard a loud knock at the front door. Frightened that it might be soldiers, Nel followed her father as he answered the summons. A stranger was standing outside, holding the hugest loaf of fresh-baked bread that Nel had ever seen. "I have orders to deliver this to you, Mr. Van Schaik," the man announced. "And a very good evening to you!"

Astonished, the family gave thanks, not only for the bread but for the faith they shared.

But that faith, in the Reformed Calvinist Church, was also a source of confusion for Nel. She was being raised to believe that God had two Official Books. In one was the names of those people predestined to go to hell; in the other, the names of those selected for heaven. "No one could alter anything in this setup—it stood fixed and finished," Nel recalls. "I was told to be a good girl, and when I died, I would discover where I belong." This theory didn't seem right, the child thought. But who was she to question it?

Eventually the Van Schaiks emigrated to Pretoria, South Africa, where they attended the Afrikaans-speaking Reformed Church. Nel met and married her husband, G. J. (Roelie) Roeleveld, and the couple had three children. "We remained active in the Reformed Church," Nel relates. "But as time passed, we felt less comfortable there. Roelie and I were repeatedly accused of not being 'good Christians,' because we sent our children to English-speaking schools. This shook us a bit, because we could not imagine God having likes or dislikes regarding nationality and language."

Nel began to long for *real* answers about God. One night she had a dreamlike experience. Someone, a gentle, fatherly figure, was standing by her bedside. He bent low so Nel could see His face. It was full of goodness, holiness, and strength, and He seemed to know her very well. Nel was filled with joy and recognition. "Are you the Lord?" she asked.

He was. Somehow, He conveyed it to her. He put his hand on her forehead in a gesture of blessing and did the same to her husband sleeping next to her. Blissfully Nel fell into a sound slumber.

She told no one of this experience. "But a ray of light, like a laser beam, had penetrated my thinking," Nel says. "Perhaps there was more to be known about Christianity than I had ever thought possible." She began to pray that God might guide her to a church community that would nourish and teach her more about Him.

Eventually Nel and her family joined an English-speaking Methodist church, where the hymns and teachings stirred her heart. "Here I learned that God kept only one book, in which names of many people were written down, and there was room for everybody," she says. "Every time a name was added, God and His angels rejoiced. Yet the book contained many blank pages. This was because, before your name could be added, you had to make a personal decision to follow the Lord all the way."

As time passed, Nel made that decision. She read the Bible and worked more diligently on her own faults. She and her husband and children were all baptized, and the family visited Pentecostal church services to learn more about the gifts of the Holy Spirit. Eventually, the family began to pray in tongues, which deepened everyone's spiritual life. At times, Nel felt she was being readied for some kind of *mission*. But what? And why would God choose a housewife living in a small village at the southern tip of South Africa—virtually the end of the earth—to work for Him? Nel had sought God almost completely on her own. But now she needed a definite answer from above. Was she on the right path? Did He have a specific job for her? "God, give me a sign," Nel often prayed.

At this point, Nel's older daughter Charlotte wanted a bedroom of her own. "We had a little storeroom available in a corner of the house," Nel says. "Roelie added a window to it, and Charlotte was happy with it."

Until winter came. Then, two sides of the room began to glisten with water. "I had forgotten that these walls had leaked from rain and condensation for the seven years we'd been in the house," Nel recalls. "It hadn't mattered so much when it was a storeroom." But now, as it took two huge towels to wipe down the walls each morning, Nel thought there must be a better way.

Was this the kind of thing she should ask God about? Or was it too small, insulting the magnificence of the Almighty? Why should He be concerned with her water problem? And yet Nel remembered the loaf of bread so unexpectedly delivered when she was a child, the vision of Love Himself one night as she slept. . . .

Nel knelt down by Charlotte's bed. She would mention the walls very briefly, she decided. But, "while praying, I was astonished by an awareness of a Presence standing to my left, just inside the room," she remembers. "Somehow the Presence told me to actually put my hands on those walls and to pray over them in tongues."

Was it an angel? Nel thought she must be imagining things, because the request seemed so odd. She started to pray again, timidly. "Lord, You can fix the walls, and they do need fixing . . ."

But again she sensed the same message. God wanted her to participate in His work, to take authority over problems with confidence. *Get up and go to the wall.* Well, she *was* alone. No one would know. . . . Nel went and placed her hands on the walls, touching them in several places. "I commanded them to dry up in the name of Jesus," she says. "Then I prayed in tongues, thanked the Lord for this miracle, and hung the wet towels outside to dry."

The next morning, as she entered Charlotte's room, Nel held her breath. "I went up to the walls, felt them, looked, then stared. The walls were perfectly dry." Nel pulled Charlotte's bed away from the walls. The area behind it was dry as well.

Nel said nothing to her family. What if the whole thing was a coincidence? The following day the family left on vacation for several weeks.

When they returned in the pouring rain, they met their neighbor. "I hope you had nice weather," he said, "because here it's been raining steadily every day for two weeks."

Charlotte's room would be flooded, Nel thought as she hurried into the house, leaving a trail of holiday baggage in her wake. But no. Astonished, she gazed at the walls. They were completely dry, as if they had bathed in two weeks of sunshine instead of streaming rainwater.

On another occasion, Nel needed a sweater from her closet after she had already put her then-infant son Martin to bed in his crib in their room. Not wanting to turn on a light and awaken him, Nel felt her way in the darkness, retrieved the sweater, and was almost out the door when she heard a strange rasping sound coming from the baby's crib.

Instantly Nel switched on the light and noticed that baby Martin seemed to be having trouble breathing.

The rattle! Where was the baby's rattle? Trying not to panic, Nel found the little plastic toy under the blanket and noticed that there was a thin, jagged-edged piece missing from it. The baby must have swallowed it! Forcing herself to keep calm, Nel pried open Martin's mouth, but she could see nothing. And yet the baby's frightening, raspy breathing continued. The piece must have been stuck much farther down than Nel could see.

By now, Martin's skin was turning an unhealthy purple hue, and he was beginning to choke. "Lord," Nel cried out, "what do I do? How do I pray?"

Take authority . . . Again, she remembered. God had not left His children helpless in this world. He had given them dominion over all things, if they would but pray that His power be given to them. A calmness came over Nel as she reached for the baby and put him in a sitting position. Then she spoke, with strength, to that fragment of plastic. "In the name of Jesus, come out of my baby now. Come out!"

Immediately, Martin let out a huge burp, and something red appeared in his mouth. Was he bleeding? No, it was the piece of missing plastic! She opened Martin's mouth, took out the plastic, gave the baby a drink, and put him back to sleep.

"No, Charlotte's little room did not become a shrine," Nel says today. "But it never leaked again." Nor did baby Martin suffer any ill effects from what could have been a tragedy. And Nel, who had come face-to-face with the results of acts of faith, had no doubt that God was going to use her in His work, again and again, whenever she asked. Today she and Roelie lead a busy and spiritually based life helping others, with plenty of time for prayer. All that is needed to work in God's kingdom, she has learned, is a willing heart—and the courage to ask for miracles.

Miracle on the Mountain

[Miracles] are designed with one goal in mind: to bring glory to God.

—JODIE BERNDT
CELEBRATION OF MIRACLES

God communicates with us in many ways—through healings, inner stirrings, challenges to our faith, and even visions and dreams. Sometimes these events seek to reassure us or warn us of impending danger. But for Jackie Greaves, there had been no indication of the nightmare to come. Surely not when she and two men friends set off to climb the 4,000-foot

Cairngorm Derry, one of Scotland's highest mountain peaks, where conditions can sometimes be as treacherous as the Himalayas. Far from being intimidated, Jackie, a fifty-two-year-old school secretary and grandmother from Warrington, England, was looking forward to the venture. She had hiked on mountains for many years, though she hadn't done much climbing until recently. But she was always careful and well prepared. For this trip she had packed a rucksack containing emergency food and some survival supplies and dressed warmly. Her companions, both teachers at the school where she worked, were younger and even more experienced than she. What could go wrong?

The trio biked up the hilly terrain for the first three miles, then chained the bikes and continued on foot. It was a typical cold, clear Sunday in February 1994, and despite the exertion, Jackie felt exhilarated. *There's something to be said for conquering the elements,* she thought. With any luck, they'd soon be at the top of this peak!

They had just stopped to share some sandwiches, at about 2:00 P.M., when gale-force winds seemed to come from nowhere. "They whipped up the snow, creating a whiteout, and we could hardly see our hands in front of our faces," Jackie says. The three knew they had to get back to safety as soon as possible. Carefully they started to turn . . . then suddenly, the cliff on which they were standing gave way! In a cloud of snow, Jackie's companions vanished. Screaming, Jackie herself hurtled down the side of the wall.

"The fall was terrifying, and it seemed to go on for ages," she says. "I was holding my ice ax and I managed to swing it into the side of the cliff as I was falling." The ice caught the ax, pulling it out of her hands but slowing her tumble, and she was able to dig her heels into the slippery side. She had stopped!

Slowly Jackie scraped out enough snow to make a hole, then wriggled into a sitting position inside. The blizzard was still too thick for her to see anything. She was alive—bruised but uninjured as far as she could tell—but where was she? Probably right above a plateau, she surmised; she had fallen awfully far. "Dave!" she shouted. "Bruce, are you there?" No response came except the whistle of the wind.

Then the whiteout cleared for just a moment, and Jackie's terror increased. She wasn't anywhere *near* a plateau, she saw. No, there were hundreds of feet of . . . nothing . . . beneath her! She was hanging almost vertically on the side of this precipice. Any moment now, her precarious position could give way, and she would crash downward again, perhaps to her death.

The whiteout closed around her once more. Jackie sat, as an hour passed, perhaps two. Periodically she would blow her whistle six times—the universal distress signal—but no one responded. She had never felt so lonely in all her life, except for the tragic period six years earlier when her eighteen-year-old daughter, Lesley, had died in a car accident. That was when Jackie had turned away from God. Admittedly, she had never been a very spiritual person. But there was no reason to pray to Someone who would take such a wonderful person as Lesley.

Now, however, as the snow whirled about

her, Jackie wished she had faith. Maybe God would listen after all.

Wait! Jackie looked up. Was that a light above? Yes, something white and clear, shining like a flashlight through the now-darkening mist. Was another climber coming to rescue her? "Bruce! Dave! Here I am!" Jackie shouted, and frantically blew her whistle. No one answered, nor did the light move. But as night fell and the snow continued to blow, the inexplicable glow remained.

Sunday evening, 9:00 P.M. Eight police officers, fourteen volunteers, and a helicopter on standby had assembled at the base of the Cairngorm Mountains, alerted by Jackie's friend Bruce, who had managed to reach help. The team would split into two groups and start their climb, looking for Dave and Jackie. "If they're dressed warmly enough and not injured, they may survive," one rescuer told another.

"Right," the other responded. "Unless this blizzard keeps up."

———

The blizzard kept up. For seventeen hours, Jackie lay at an angle against the side of the mountain, too frightened to move, while sixty-mile-an-hour winds buffeted her slight figure. Shivering, teeth chattering, she reviewed her life and thought about her two remaining children and her beloved grandchildren. She ate snow and wished she felt secure enough to open her rucksack and put on her remaining clothes. But if she slipped . . . Terror rose, then subsided, as calm once again moved over her. There was no need to panic, for she was not alone. Hundreds of feet above her, unmoving, like a watchful beacon, the mysterious light continued to shine. Where had it come from? And why did it stay?

About 6:00 A.M., as the area around her grew brighter, Jackie realized that the beam was dimming. Soon it disappeared. She was still wrapped in whirling snow, stiff and almost frozen, but during these desolate hours on the side of the mountain, she had come to a decision. She could either die here, waiting for rescuers who would probably never find her, or she could risk climbing farther down and possibly falling. "I hacked out a place in the ice with my toe, slid down on my stomach, hacked out another place with the other foot and decided to keep going," she says. Her plan worked. By 7:30 A.M. she had reached the plateau far beneath her, now piled high with snowdrifts. She managed to open the frozen zipper on her rucksack and pull on the extra clothing she had brought. But what next? The cold was terrible, the wind still fierce, there was white above her, white beneath her—what direction should she go in?

It was impossible. She couldn't go anywhere or make any more decisions, not without God. She had tried so long to ignore Him, but it just hadn't worked. "God," she heard herself say, "I don't know why this is happening, or where I'm going, but You're my only hope. Please don't leave me."

Strange. She thought she heard someone calling, a man's voice. But it was coming from far below. How could that be—wasn't she at the bottom of the mountain by now? It must be her imagination. Struggling against the gusts, and drifts taller than she was, Jackie put one painful foot in front of the other, again and again and again. *God, don't leave me. Don't leave me . . .*

She had been walking for hours, it seemed, when she heard it. *Stop.* Almost a whisper, a dream-word, but not quite. Why, there was a barrier in front of her. Jackie squinted against the white surroundings. It was a railroad crossing bar! But that was impossible—there were no railroad tracks here. Jackie leaned out to touch it, and it disappeared. Was she hallucinating? But, wait! Jackie almost screamed. A huge hole lay ahead, right where she had been about to step. She could see down into it, hundreds of feet below. She wasn't at the *bottom* of the mountain, as she had presumed. No, she was on another ledge, and she could plunge through it again, just as she had earlier.

Terror-stricken, Jackie turned to her right and took a step. Immediately, a second railroad barrier slid down directly in front of her. Again she stopped, and the barrier vanished. Beyond it she saw another wide hole.

Turning, Jackie went back the way she had come. She felt a strong Presence. Someone was definitely with her. Someone had just saved her from death.

It had been a long, frustrating day, Willie Fraser decided as he and Solo, his German shepherd, drove home. Appalling weather conditions had forced one of the search parties to dig in and remain on the mountaintop last night, but the second team had searched until dawn. They had found the man safe and well, and that was something to be grateful for. But they had not yet found Mrs. Greaves. (The searchers would later learn that Jackie's companions, disoriented by the whiteout, had given the rescue teams incorrect directions as to where she might be.)

Willie and Solo, along with seventy others, had looked for almost ten hours today. At one point, Willie had glanced up through whirling snow to a plateau just above and thought he had seen something moving. But when he shouted, the wind had swept his words away.

Solo had already rescued three people this winter. She was the best dog ever—gentle and sweet-natured yet brave. If the lost lady was still out there, Solo could find her. Willie went home to his own young family with a grateful heart and renewed determination. Tomorrow was another day.

Jackie was in another land, a beautiful place. . . . She had traveled through some kind of tunnel and seemed to be floating. The terrain around her was beautiful, all blue and white and warm, with trees, flowers, Japanese-style bridges, and the same strong Presence that had been with her since her ordeal on the mountain began. Was she in heaven?

No. She was in the mysterious tunnel again, then back in her body, back in this horror that wouldn't end. . . . Perhaps this night on the mountain would be her last, but she wasn't alone. Once again the Presence had reassured her, given her the will to hold on just a while longer. She wouldn't go to sleep tonight.

With frozen hands, Jackie dug a "snow hole," curled up inside her torn survival bag, and talked to herself. "I sang silly songs, made up stories, thought about the past—just like the

night before," she says. "Most of all, I prayed."
Perhaps she would meet God soon. She wanted
to spend some time thinking about Him, time
she wished she had shared with Him all along.

Morning came, but it brought yet another
alarm. Snow blindness. "My eyes were barely
working," Jackie says, "but I could see that I was
surrounded by five-foot walls of snow that the
wind had blown around me. There was just a
little daylight showing on top." Would it cave in
on her before she could escape? Using the last of
her strength, Jackie struggled up the frozen
walls, watching helplessly as the shreds of her
survival bag blew away. She wouldn't live
through another night without it. Clambering to
her feet, she looked around. Still a whiteout, still
no sense of direction. What should she do?

Again a light! It shone against the white like
a V, then vanished. Jackie put her compass position on where the light had been. *Don't go,
Light.* . . . She started toward it, sliding, stag-
gering, now falling down a steep hill, tumbling,
tumbling . . .

"Solo! Come back!" Willie and his dog had been searching since dawn and had gotten far ahead of their team. He couldn't blame the dog for being eager, but it was best to stay with the group.

But now Solo streaked through the snow, head back, mouth open. She had picked up a scent. Yes! There was someone ahead! Solo ran toward the figure, then darted back to get Willie. From behind them a chorus of barking erupted. Other dogs had caught the scent and were racing forward. "Are you Jackie?" Willie shouted as he ran toward the small, slight figure.

"Yes! Yes, thank God!" The woman had fallen in a heap and was reaching out to hug the dogs as they circled her, yelping in delight. Willie ran to her, as members of his search party shouted the news to one another.

It was 9:20 A.M. Jackie Greaves's forty-two-hour ordeal was over.

"She's a remarkably brave and fortunate lady," surgeon Mark Janssens reported to the *Daily Mail* after treating Jackie at Raigmore Hospital.

"She required very little treatment; she had slight frostbite on her fingers, but otherwise she was unhurt." No hypothermia, no lasting effects from dehydration or snow blindness? People all over the country were amazed; there was talk of little else for days. Some stopped short of calling it a miracle. But Jackie has no such reluctance.

"God had His hand on me all through this ordeal, from the mysterious light to the railroad barriers that prevented me from falling—even to the awareness that I was not alone," she says today. "And the experience has changed my life." Jackie now spends much of her time visiting the sick, raising money for charity, helping children who need extra attention, and giving back to God the great gift He has given her. The gift of survival, of course. But most important, the gift of Himself.

Janie's Vision

> *Vision is the art of seeing things invisible.*
>
> —*JONATHAN SWIFT*
> *"THOUGHTS ON VARIOUS SUBJECTS"*

It was one of those landmark events, a ritual being repeated in households all over Omaha, Nebraska, and around the country, too: the first day of school. Janie Murnane's oldest son, Jeff, was about to embark on his great adventure, and Janie was having a little trouble letting go.

It wasn't that her almost-six-year-old wasn't prepared. "We had decided that Jeff was responsible enough to walk to school by himself," Janie explains, "so we had practiced traveling the ten-block route to school many times. Sometimes Patty Ann, his best friend, came along, and sometimes it was just us. Not only could Jeff lead the way, he usually tugged at me when I slowed down on the hills." The route *was* long, and at the time there was one busy four-lane intersection—Saddle Creek and Hamilton Streets—in a commercial area. But Jeff had been drilled, over and over again, on how to cross that street, by waiting for the WALK sign. He was a reliable child, and Janie knew he would be careful. Still, she was worried.

Now, however, as Jeff dressed excitedly in his new school clothes, ate a hasty breakfast, and grabbed his schoolbag, Janie was caught up in his joy. She said good-bye to her younger son, who would be spending his own special day at a friend's house, then followed Jeff out the front door. "Jeff, slow down!"

Jeff barely turned around. "Bye, Daisy!" He waved to the family dog. "I've got to go to school today!"

Janie caught up to him and took his hand.

"You'll be careful, won't you, honey? Especially when you get to Saddle Creek . . ."

"Uh-huh." Jeff had heard it all before. As Patty Ann came racing out of her house, Jeff pulled away. "See you later, Mom!" he called, running to meet his friend.

Janie watched the children wistfully until they were out of sight. The end of an era . . . Was she happy or sad about it? A little of both, she decided, as she turned back to face the household chores.

The day passed uneventfully, except for the unaccustomed silence surrounding her. It was later on, toward the time Jeff should be starting home, that Janie began to feel uneasy. Something was wrong. She couldn't describe it, just . . . wrong.

Ridiculous. She was probably nervous because Jeff would have to cross that intersection again, at an even busier time of day. Hadn't she already told herself a hundred times that this apprehension was normal—and something she'd just have to get over?

A chill ran down her spine. No, it was more than anxiety. This nameless dread was growing.

But why? Now an all-encompassing sense of danger, fear, even loss, rolled over her. Her heart began to pound and terror engulfed her. Something was going to happen to Jeff if she didn't stop it! Overwhelmed, Janie raced out her front door.

As she ran, the scene in front of her eyes began to change. Although she was on her familiar street, Janie was actually seeing—and hearing—something else. A truck! Yes, she could see it—not as something real but as a vision. Yet the sense of imminent danger, of horror, was all around her. "The truck was speeding, bursting through an intersection," Janie recalls. "I could hear children laughing and shouting, the sounds of traffic getting louder, then tires screeching, children screaming . . ."

Janie had never experienced anything like this. *God, God.* Her prayer welled from deep inside as she gasped for air and kept running. Saddle Creek and Hamilton. Something she could not understand was occurring there. *God, give me courage. Help us.*

Blocks sped by, houses passed. Janie was getting winded. Her legs ached, but fear drove her on. And then, yes, the vision was receding; Janie was approaching the actual intersection. There were Jeff and Patty Ann! They were crossing the first half of the street, walking toward the median, laughing and talking. The WALK sign facing them was on, cars had stopped, everything seemed normal. Yet Janie was still frantic, the peril around her acute and horrible . . .

There was a truck, speeding toward the intersection! At the same moment, Jeff and Patty Ann stepped down from the median to cross the second half of the street. "Jeff!" Janie screamed, waving her arms as she ran. "Stop! Stop!"

The traffic noise was drowning out her words. The children took another step into the path of the truck. Then Jeff looked up and saw Janie at the curb. "Wait!" She held up her hands. Instantly he stopped.

The scene seemed to be frozen—except for the truck. Brakes screeching, it swerved wildly, just missing the children, and continued on. But they were safe! Janie had reached the intersection just in time.

"Mommy!" Jeff finished crossing the street,

ran to Janie, and threw his arms around her. "Mommy, why are you crying?"

Several years later, Janie still finds it difficult to describe or explain this odd warning, but she is certain it was more than just an active imagination. "I've since had many premonitions that dealt with Jeff and imminent danger," she says. "Once I felt compelled to run to the park, and I discovered that he had fallen from a slide and broken his arm. Jeff has also overcome some health problems, and God was with us during those trying times too." Janie realized long ago that her children belong to God and are in His hands. Perhaps He is alerting her to dangers because He has more in store for them here on earth and somehow needs her help to protect them. Perhaps Janie hears the warnings because she is willing to listen.

Whatever the answers, she knows He is near. "Our family is precious," she says, "and we thank Him every day for the love, joy, and laughter we share."

Heavenly Dream

Oh dream, how sweet, too sweet,
too bitter sweet,
Whose wakening should have been
in Paradise.

—*CHRISTINA ROSSETTI*

"ECHO"

Not all of God's visions and dreams are dramatic. In some, He simply shows His tenderness.

On June 30, 1994, Elizabeth Kingsbury-Puscas's father-in-law, Victor Puscas, died of cancer. He had been a beloved husband and father to his five children and a vigorous, respected chief of police in Aurora, Illinois. Elizabeth's husband, Vic, the youngest and his dad's name-sake, had been a police officer too for a while, before eventually becoming a lawyer. "I was close to my father-in-law; he was probably my favorite relative on my husband's side of the family and an all-around fun man, loved by many," Elizabeth recalls. "We were all there when he died, and we grieved deeply."

Several weeks later, Elizabeth had a strange dream. "I dreamed I got stung by a bee," she says. "While it may not seem important to most people, to me it was terrifying, because I'd never been stung before, and I know that our family has bad reactions to stings." Nothing frightening happened in the dream itself. But the next day, as Elizabeth visited her parents out on their deck, a bee actually did sting her! "Although I was very frightened, I didn't have as bad a reaction as I had anticipated," she says. "My forearm was swollen just like Popeye's, but ointment was all we really needed to bring the swelling down."

Elizabeth remained a bit leery of bees, but almost forgot the incident until a few weeks later, when she had another dream. "In this dream, someone told me that I could visit my father-in-law," she recalls, "and I was so excited and happy, even though I somehow understood that the visit would be a short one."

Then, in the dream, Elizabeth found herself in a grassy area near a beautiful beach. It was a parklike setting, with mature shade trees along the edge where the grass and sand met. It was a very sunny day, with a few clouds in a brilliant blue sky, and pleasantly warm.

There was her father-in-law, sitting on a concrete bench. But he was not alone. Next to him was his wife. Elizabeth assumed the couple would appreciate a little time together before she approached the bench, so she stayed to the side, kneeling in the grass and watching the scene. "Dad was telling Mom one of his famous stories—laughing as always," she recalls. "However, he was also playing with a beautiful little girl with long dark hair and straight bangs. She was about four. She'd laugh, get close enough to him for him to tickle her, dash away, then giggle and go back for more." Was she one of the family nieces? No. When Elizabeth looked closer, she realized she had never seen this child before. Who was she?

Elizabeth sensed that Victor knew she was there kneeling in the grass. But abruptly, without either speaking to the other, the dream ended. Elizabeth was disappointed that it hadn't lasted longer, but the experience left her with such a feeling of love and consolation that she told her husband about it as soon as he awakened. He was as pleased as Elizabeth was.

That evening, Vic spoke with his mother on the phone. When he hung up, he looked at Elizabeth, puzzled. "Mom finally had a dream about Dad last night," he told Elizabeth.

"Really? I'm so glad." Elizabeth knew her mother-in-law had been hoping for such an occurrence.

"Elizabeth, it was the *same* dream as yours. She was sitting on a bench talking with him, you were kneeling in the grass watching them, and he was playing with a little girl that she didn't recognize—a girl with long dark hair and straight bangs."

Elizabeth was astonished. She knew that God

often spoke to His children through dreams. But what was He saying? Was this meant as a comforting message, that Victor was indeed safely home in heaven? If so, was that the *only* message?

Apparently not. For, just a month later, Elizabeth discovered that she was expecting. And on May 31, 1995, her daughter arrived, a baby with dark straight hair and a very familiar face. "Why, this is the child in the dream," Vic's mother told the couple as soon as she'd seen the infant. Somehow, they were not surprised.

Nor did it seem odd that, just before their daughter's birth, Vic and Elizabeth were cleaning out a closet and came upon a Bible that Vic had once used. Flipping through it, he found a prayer card of St. Michael the Archangel. "Did you put this here?" he asked Elizabeth. But she had never seen the card before. "Michael is the patron saint of police officers, so we figured Dad had sent the picture, still 'in on things' from heaven," Elizabeth says. "So that's why we named the baby Michaela (mi-KAY-la)." And as their daughter grows, Elizabeth and Vic do their best to tell her about her *mosiu* (MO-shew), the Romanian word for "grandfather."

God's ways are not always our ways, and that's why Elizabeth has thought frequently about these unusual episodes. "It seems to me that the dream about the bee sting was God's way of saying, 'Pay attention—something I show you is about to come true,' " Elizabeth says. "Perhaps this is why I then took the dream about my father-in-law so seriously. People ask me now if I feel bad about not being able to see my daughter play with my father-in-law, because he was so good with children.

"I tell them I have already seen them together. What a gift."

Soldier to the Rescue

*Character is what you are in
the dark.*

—DWIGHT L. MOODY
SERMONS: CHARACTER

Steve Campbell still cannot explain why he
made a decision that could have ended in
dangerous consequences. "You do what you
have to do," he says simply.

Steve, a soldier stationed at Fort Bragg,
North Carolina, was preparing to take his three
children on a 650-mile drive to his parents'
house for Thanksgiving. Unfortunately, his wife

couldn't come because she had to work. "During the time we've lived at Fort Bragg, I've made the trip to my folks' house in Radcliff, Kentucky, several times, both day and night," Steve says. So he knows the roads well and wasn't concerned about driving as night turned into Thanksgiving morning.

But this time he had taken the family van, which uses gas more quickly than their other car. "I noticed on the outskirts of Lexington, Kentucky, about 2:30 A.M., that I was getting low and ought to stop for gas," Steve says. "But the last open station I passed in Lexington was on the other side of the highway, with a median between us, and I didn't want to stop and turn around." He'd be heading onto the Bluegrass Parkway, he knew, and there would be one open oasis after another. He'd watch for the next one.

But to Steve's mounting concern, each rest area that he passed was closed and darkened. He belatedly realized that because it was a holiday, nothing would be open. This was a bad situation. There was no way he was going to get to his parents' house now; his gauge had been on

E for some time already. It was unusually cold that night, and although the children were snug under the few blankets he'd brought along, what would happen if the car ran out of gas and the heater went off? He hadn't seen another car in miles, and he knew this stretch of highway had few if any houses on it. And when the van eventually ran out of gas—well, Steve was a big man and a tough G.I. But would he be able to protect all three of his children if they were set upon by criminals?

Although sputtering, the van continued to travel. Oddly, it had gone more than 100 miles since Lexington, Steve realized; he wouldn't have thought he could have gotten that far. And then his luck finally ran out. The engine died, and the van coasted to a stop on a desolate stretch of road, with no highway lights to show them where they were and no drivers with cell phones to flag down.

Steve switched off the headlights and opened the door. Might as well see where he was. Maybe there was a house nearby.

It was then that he heard it. A woman's voice, calling weakly. "Help. Help me."

It must be his imagination. Who would be out here at four-thirty in the morning?

"Help." The plea came again. It sounded like it was somewhere below him.

Thoughts flooded his mind. It could be someone in distress . . . or a trap, with thugs waiting for him to go down a pitch-dark embankment so they could ambush and mug him. How could he leave the kids alone in the car while he went to investigate? But how could he walk away from someone who might be hurt or even dying?

He made his decision quickly, taking several road flares and setting them up behind his van to protect it. He grabbed a flashlight. "Watch my light," he told his oldest son. "If it goes out, you'll know I've been mugged. Then turn the flares off and lock the van doors." Steve went to the edge of the road and sent the thin stream of light downward. There, in a ditch about twenty feet below, was a crumpled car. "It could barely be seen unless you were standing right over it," he says. "A casual passerby would have never noticed it."

"Help me," the voice cried again. It was coming from the car.

Swiftly Steve scrambled down the bluff. The car was overturned and coated with ice—it looked, he thought, as if it had been abandoned there for months. Yet he had heard that voice. He peered inside the wreckage, but no one was there. "Hello?" he called. "Where are you?"

"Here," came the voice. Steve circled the car and finally found a young woman lying on her side in the frozen mud, her hips and legs pinned under the car. She had been trapped there, she whispered, since she'd lost control of her car and it went over the side of the ditch, about eight hours earlier. No one had heard her cries. The temperature was now twenty-five degrees.

Steve took a few moments to reassure her. "I thought I better not try and move her—I might do more harm than good," he says. But when he heard the sound of a truck rumbling down the highway, he ran back up the hill and flagged it down with his flashlight. While the trucker called for help on his CB radio, Steve grabbed his jack and the blankets, clambered back down the embankment, used the jack to lift the car off the victim, and kept her as warm as possible. Within thirty minutes the woman was being loaded into a rescue helicopter. Steve learned later that she had suffered several broken bones but would recover.

One of the officials at the scene saw to it that Steve got some gas, and the Campbells continued on their way. "I honestly didn't think anything more about it," Steve says, "until later that day. My mother thanked God at our Thanksgiving meal for bringing me there at the right time to help that lady." Then Steve started to think a little harder. Given the fact that the distance between his parents' house and his is 650 miles, and given the fact that the van seemed to travel longer than usual on E, what were the odds that Steve would run out of gas at the exact spot where a young woman was in desperate need of help?

"Maybe that lady's guardian angel took care of it all," Steve muses. But not without an earthly angel who was asked to accept a mission—and said yes.

Delilah's Prayer

*Yet He commanded the skies above,
and the doors of heaven He
opened; He rained manna upon
them for food and gave them
heavenly bread.*

—PSALMS 78:23–24

Children don't worry about their relationship with God as much as we adults do. They accept the fact that they can ask for even the most glorious things, and God can do it, if He chooses. Brother Leo Keigher, who has worked with the poor all over the world, remembers a little Guatemalan girl named Delilah. "Delilah, who was about eight or nine when I knew her, was a very spiritual child," says Brother Leo, "and would never have told me anything but the absolute truth." Once Delilah came to him to report on a wondrous event that had just occurred.

Delilah was the oldest of several children whose father had deserted them. The family lived in a small shanty with one bed and a table and chairs as their only furniture. Their ingenious mother supported them by making lunches, which she then took to nearby factories and sold to the workers there. While her mother was gone, Delilah or one of the neighbors would watch her younger children. "After my mother sells all the lunches, she has enough money to buy ingredients for the next day's lunches and the beans for our supper that night," Delilah once explained to Brother Leo.

The system was working very well, and one day as Delilah's mother loaded up her cart to make the trip to town, she called to Delilah. "Today I have left beans simmering for our supper in the fireplace," she told her daughter.

"So early?" Delilah asked.

"I have chores to do in town after I sell the

lunches," her mother explained. "I won't be back right away. But you know how to stir the beans so they won't stick to the kettle."

Delilah nodded. She had done it a few times. She was a little afraid of the open fire, but she had never let her mother know.

"And you will keep the younger children away from the flames so that no one gets hurt," her mother instructed.

"Yes, Mother." Delilah nodded and watched as her mother, pulling the cart, walked down the dusty road toward town. Then she took the children outside to play for a while, so they would be less likely to trip and fall into the flames.

As the time passed, Delilah looked into the shanty several times and began to grow concerned. The flames seemed to be getting higher under the pot, and the beans were bubbling faster and faster. Standing on her tiptoes, Delilah stirred the mixture, but she didn't know how to make it quiet down like her mother did. She went to the door uncertainly, watching the younger ones play. What should she do?

Just then, Delilah heard a *wham!* Then

another. She whirled. Oh, no! The pot had cracked, once, twice—no, many times—and beans were running down onto the fire, across the floor. More beans flew into the room, coating the bed and table. . . . The fire sizzled, filling the little shanty with smoke. It was a mess! But, worse, there was nothing left for supper.

"Oh, dear God." Delilah went outside and fell on her knees. "What am I going to do? Because of me, our best kettle—and our supper—is ruined. My mother is going to be so angry! Please help me!"

She looked up. There was her mother, hurrying down the path toward them. Delilah grabbed the younger children, brought them into the shanty, pushed them under the bed, and slid in next to them.

"Why are we under the bed?" her younger sister asked. "Ugh—it's wet in here!"

"Delilah! Where is everyone?" Her mother called as she came into the hut.

"We're under the bed," Delilah answered, waiting for her mother to scream as she saw the ruined mess all over the room.

"Under the bed? Well, come out! The beans

will be ready in just a few minutes now, and you can have your supper."

The beans? What was wrong with her mother? Hadn't she seen the pot, split in pieces from the too-high temperature, the liquid everywhere? Slowly Delilah crawled out from under the bed, her eyes riveted on the fireplace. There was the pot, intact, hanging from the hook like it always did. Inside were the beans, looking like they always did, filling the family's humble home with fragrance. Supper was indeed ready.

Delilah never hesitated to ask God for miracles—large and small—after that. She had learned that nothing was too little for Him to care about. Not even beans.

Guardian on the Bench

But if these beings guard you, they do so because they have been summoned by your prayers.

—ST. AMBROSE, FOURTH CENTURY

Kathy Smith is now a wife and mom in East Fallowfield, Pennsylvania, but one summer when she was younger, she lived with a group of girlfriends in Margate City, New Jersey, and worked in Atlantic City. She took public transportation for her daily twenty-minute commute.

Kathy was just getting adjusted to her job when workers in Atlantic City declared a transit strike. So she started taking a cab each morning to the boundary of Atlantic City, then waited for a company shuttle bus to pick up employees.

It was becoming rather complicated when a coworker offered to give Kathy a ride. "I pick up several other girls on my way to work—it's no problem," she assured Kathy.

"Really? That would be great! Where should we meet?"

"Let's see . . . I go right by the corner of Atlantic Avenue and White Horse Pike. That's not far from where you live. Just be sure you're there at six-thirty."

"I will be," Kathy assured her.

The following day Kathy arrived at the intersection of Atlantic and White Horse a little early so as not to miss her ride. She had never noticed, from the bus, how absolutely deserted and quiet the area was at this hour. "The whole city was like a ghost town," she recalls. "No one walking anywhere, no traffic, no businesses open . . ."

Abruptly, there was a loud commotion in the distance. A car came speeding down the street, with six or seven teenage boys yelling and swearing out the open windows. The noise echoed through the silent area. They were obviously drunk, perhaps just coming home from a party. As they raced past her, several yelled rude remarks. Kathy ignored them and tried to look inconspicuous. But how? "There was no place to hide—the area was wide open, and no one was out there but me," she says. "If I left, I'd miss my ride, and besides, where would I go? Anyone could have grabbed me at any time." She sat down on a bench set several feet back from the curb. Maybe the boys would just go on home.

No. She heard the muffler and the tires shrieking as the gang drove around the block again. This time the car slowed in front of her, and two of the youths leaned out, shouting and leering, before they accelerated again. "Oh, God . . ." Kathy began to pray. Why hadn't some resident been awakened by now and called the police?

When Kathy heard the car coming around the block for the third time, she began to panic. This time it stopped in front of her. "Hey, girl! Get in! Get in!" several of the boys shouted, while the others laughed. They were obviously intoxicated or high on drugs.

What should she do? If she tried to run, they could certainly catch up with her. Still no traffic, no police, no other people . . . "Dear God, please help me," she whispered.

Unexpectedly, from somewhere behind her, a young man approached. "Hi." He smiled. "Have you been waiting long?" He sat down right next to Kathy and slid his arm across the back of the bench.

"He was dressed like a tourist, wearing a bright flowered Hawaiian shirt and shorts," Kathy recalls. "He was clean-cut, with the most beautiful eyes I've ever seen." But rather than relax, she was immediately even more frightened. Was he part of the gang in the car that was still idling at the curb? No, she thought; he was obviously sober, and his behavior was quite different.

"Just act like you know me," the young man said quietly.

Kathy was confused. "Who are you?" she whispered.

"Hey, girl, get in the car!" One of the boys

shouted again. Now there were two in trouble, Kathy realized. This carful of thugs could easily overpower her and this nice young man.

However, he got up, turning once to smile at her, walked casually over to the car, leaned into the front window, and spoke to the group. Kathy could not hear what he was saying, but she kept looking for a policeman to break up the brawl that was sure to follow at any moment. But the next thing she knew, the car and its occupants, all strangely subdued, drove away, and the nice young man came back to sit with her on the bench.

"What . . . what did you say to them?" Kathy asked, astonished.

Her rescuer just shrugged. "They won't be back, don't worry," he said.

An awkward silence fell. Kathy was aware that something about this scenario was very unusual, but she couldn't quite figure it out. "Are you on your way to work?" she asked, for want of more interesting conversation.

"You could say that," he nodded.

"Who do you work for?" Kathy asked.

"I work for the Father," was his answer.

Surely he meant *his* father. "What does your father do?" she inquired.

"Our Father does everything," he said, smiling at her again.

The conversation was making no sense to Kathy. And there, coming down the street, was her ride. She waved for the girls to stop and jumped up from the bench. "Good-bye!" she said to the stranger and bounced into the car.

As they pulled away from the curb, she pointed him out to her coworkers. "See that good-looking man I was talking to? The one in the flowered Hawaiian shirt? He just saved me from a carful of drunks."

"Where?" Everyone turned back to look.

"The guy sitting on the bench with me when you pulled up. Right there . . ." Kathy said, turning around to catch a last glimpse. She should have been able to see him easily, since there were still no other people on the street. But he was nowhere in sight. "How did he disappear so quickly?" she wondered aloud.

"Kathy, there was no one sitting on that bench with you when we pulled up," one of the girls pointed out.

"No, you were completely alone," said another. "And I'd certainly notice a handsome man in a Hawaiian shirt!" Everyone laughed.

Were they playing a trick on her, teasing her? But no. Kathy had sensed from the moment the encounter with the stranger began that something about it was unusual, almost . . . holy. One would have to actually go through an experience like that to understand it.

I never said thank you to him for helping me, she thought. But somehow, she's sure he knows.

Part of the Glory

He who has health has hope, and
he who has hope has everything.

—*ARABIAN PROVERB*

Some people might consider Kathy Smith's rescue a coincidence. But Father Michael Drury, among many others, doesn't believe in coincidences. He is a priest of the Oratorian Community of Monterey, California, and ministers to the needs of the people served by the Oratory, including the military community at the Presidio of Monterey. But were it not for a "coincidence" that happened to him in high school, things might have turned out quite differently for him.

Young Michael had just finished his junior year at St. Joseph's High School Seminary in Los Altos, California. That year, in addition to religion, science, history, and English, Michael had decided to learn a less conventional skill: standing on his hands. "I guess it started just as a new gymnastic talent," he recalls. "And I usually couldn't do it alone—that is, I'd have to lean my feet against a wall to get completely upright." But it was fun, and whenever the spirit moved him, Michael would find a wall and stand upside down for a while. Maybe it was a release from tension or just a way to keep in shape or do something different—whatever the reason, the teachers had more important details to worry about, and no one in authority took much notice of Michael's peculiar new habit.

During the previous school year, Michael had had a few episodes of a strange weakness. The school's doctor checked him and suspected an ulcer, but tests revealed nothing. The episodes had ceased until Michael returned home for the summer.

"I had agreed to help out at St. Kevin's parish, with the kids' programs and other things," Father Michael remembers. Work began, but after a couple of weeks, Michael's strange weakness returned. He could hardly carry folding chairs from one place to another anymore. His worried parents alerted their physician.

Perhaps Michael was just fatigued from the last stressful weeks of school, the doctor surmised. "But if he has any headaches or nausea, call me right away," he said. "These are often symptoms of spinal meningitis."

The following day, Michael demonstrated his handstand trick for some of the impressed kids at St. Kevin's. "Almost immediately I became nauseated," he says. His parents took him to the hospital right away.

Michael did not have meningitis. But there *was* blood in his spinal fluid, so his doctor ordered a battery of tests related to the spine.

"Some of them were very painful, but the most painful part, especially for my parents, was the not knowing," he says. Michael's parents and grandmother prayed over him and brought Lourdes water for him to drink. Seminary professors and friends came to visit; priests from the seminary administered the Sacrament of the Sick. Michael prayed too. He believed in God, of course—wasn't he planning to become a priest? "But I really wasn't all that spiritual," he says now. "God was not at the center of my life but on the periphery. I didn't know if He was really a part of all this."

Almost two weeks after Michael had entered the hospital, he underwent a myelogram, in which dye is injected into the body so doctors can see one's organs on a screen. It was the last test the doctors were willing to try, but Michael's problem was finally diagnosed: He had a tumor in his spinal column.

The surgeon operated the very next day. "And it was a long surgery, some eight or nine hours," Father Michael says. "I remember seeing the doctor afterward—he told me that I was going to be okay, that the tumor had been a contained malignancy, and that he had gotten it all."

Sometime later, in the doctor's office, Michael asked more about the tumor and why it had gone undetected for so long. "Young man," the surgeon asked, "this may seem like an odd question. But had you been doing any strenuous activity before you experienced weakness and nausea?"

"You mean, like sports or something?" Michael was puzzled. All the guys his age played sports.

"Something a bit more specific, maybe something unusual . . ."

Michael pondered. "Well, I stand on my hands a lot," he ventured. "I guess that's pretty strenuous, if you stay up as long as I do."

"That's it," the physician said quietly. "That's what pulled your tumor apart and caused it to bleed. Spending time standing upside down may have saved your life."

Michael's tumor, the doctor explained, was a type which usually doesn't bleed. It had been only a few days away from embedding itself in the spinal cord in such a way that would have made it inoperable. Without having seen blood in the spinal fluid, doctors might have spent several more weeks—critical weeks—trying to find a cause for Michael's strange weakness while the tumor continued to grow unchecked.

Michael didn't know what to say. Standing on his hands had been just a game, something fun. Did God use such ordinary things to heal us?

"I wish I could say that my faith deepened immediately," Father Michael recalls. "But after cobalt-radiation treatments, life went on pretty much as usual. I recovered, went back to school, then started college. I was just happy to be back on my feet again." From time to time, he did think about the strange coincidence that had kept him alive, but when Michael was about twenty, he finally discovered the fuller, richer meaning of the experience he had had as a teenager. "The Holy Spirit was released in my life through the Charismatic Renewal in the Catholic Church. This started me on a deeper personal relationship with Jesus and an awareness of the meaning of my faith. And when that happened, all my values seemed to reverse. Things that I had once thought so essential—like having the right stereo equipment or luxury car—seemed secondary, even trivial, when compared to knowing and serving the Lord."

The experience of being saved by standing on his hands also took on a dimension of faith several years later. "I saw a short animated film called *Up Is Down*," Michael recalls. "It was about a man who travels through life standing on his head. Of course he sees the world from a completely different viewpoint than anyone else does. The movie's spiritual theme was that *anyone* would, once he or she decided to live their lives by the Beatitudes, the commandments, God's great love."

Standing on his head . . . Suddenly, in a burst of wonder, Michael understood that his own experience had been a parable too. "I adopted this symbol and its connection to standing on my hands as a way of looking at my cancer—and at life in general," he says. "When I had the tumor, I was going through life just like most people—seeing things through worldly eyes. And I could have continued doing just that." Instead, Jesus had turned him upside down—in more ways than one. "God's grace is saving my life spiritually just as those handstands saved my life physically—and now I am really living!"

Few of us can physically stand on our heads or even our hands. But Father Michael Drury believes that a new *faith* perspective is available to all of us. "We can choose to be part of the glory," he says. It's really as simple as that.

With a Little Help from Mom

Where there is great love, there are always miracles.

—*WILLA CATHER*

Early fall overlooking Virginia's Blue Ridge Mountains . . . *could there be a more beautiful season or scene?* Sondra Johnson mused as she and her husband, Larry, drove home from a shopping trip in town. It was always nice for the two of them to get away alone together, even if it was simply to do the mundane chores made necessary by their large family. Sondra glanced at her watch. Fourteen-year-old Robert was probably home by now, waiting for them to take him to football practice. And Elsie, Sondra's holstein, would need to be milked soon. Always lots of things to do on a farm, but Sondra had learned long ago to leave as much as she could in God's hands. "I was brought up praying," she says. "I can never remember when God was *not* a major part of my life."

Less than a mile to go on the curvy back road . . . Then, without warning, Larry slammed on the brakes and peered out the windshield. "There's a tree limb blocking the road," he said to Sondra. "But there's something else, too . . ."

Cautiously they got out of the car. Larry approached the limb to move it aside, then stopped. "Don't come any closer!" he warned Sondra. "It's smoldering—looks like it's been burning."

Burning? Sondra looked around. There were no flames anywhere. Then, even with the shadows obscuring their view, she saw it too: a fallen power line just ahead of the branch, bouncing and shooting sparks!

"I'll run to the Daneks' house and call the

power company," Larry decided. "You stay here and wave away any traffic." With any luck, there wouldn't be much, since this road was used mainly by local folks. But if someone were to drive or ride a bicycle into the live power line . . . Sondra did what came most naturally to her in any situation. She started to pray.

No one had yet come by when Larry returned. But Sondra had remembered something in his absence. Robert, waiting at home for his ride, was going to wonder where his parents were. Maybe they could carefully inch around the downed line and leave the scene.

No. She went back to the neighbor's house to make another phone call.

"Someone might get hurt if we're not here to warn them," she explained to Robert. "So we won't be able to pick you up for practice until the power company gets here and turns off the electricity."

Robert groaned. "Mom, I can't be late for practice. The coach will make me run laps afterward."

That was true, Sondra knew. Throughout

the whole season the coach was particularly rough on boys he thought did not live, eat, and breathe football. Robert's self-esteem was a bit shaky too; Sondra would have willingly carried him on her back to practice, if she could, to avoid having him singled out for punishment . . .

But wait, she realized. Why couldn't Robert come to *them*? She and Larry were less than a mile from their house if Robert took the shortcut through the back field, which he had done hundreds of times. It meant climbing over the five-strand barbed wire fence separating the Johnsons' property from the Daneks' farm, but Robert was an expert at that, too. "Robert, can I trust you to stay *completely* away from the road and just run to us through our back fields?" she asked. "Dad or I can turn around and take you to practice from here."

"Sure, Mom. I'll be careful."

Sondra hung up, filled with misgivings. Had she done the right thing? Walking back to the car, she prayed intensely. *God, please keep Robert and everyone else safe from danger. Surround us with protection.*

No vehicle had yet come down the road, including the electric company truck. The lethal power line continued to quiver like a lightning bolt. And where was Robert? Eight minutes . . . ten minutes . . . Sondra kept eyeing her watch. Robert was a fast runner; he had been ready to leave, and the trip was mostly downhill. What was keeping him? Had he gotten stuck on barbed wire? *God, I place him in Your hands.*

A truck approached. It was the power company. "The electricity is turned off now," the driver announced as he alighted. "Thanks for standing guard."

Sondra barely heard him for, racing down the field toward her, just as she had instructed, was her son.

Relief flooded her. "Oh, Robert, what took you so long?" she cried as he ran to her side.

"It was the barbed wire fence," Robert explained, catching his breath. "I couldn't get over it. It was the strangest thing, Mom—every time I got close enough to grab on and climb it, I felt pushed back. Like something invisible was in front of me so I couldn't touch the fence. Finally, after a few tries, I just rolled under it."

The power company worker had overheard, and his face turned pale. He walked over to Robert. "It's a good thing you didn't touch that barbed wire, son," he said. "This live power line was lying right across it. You would have been electrocuted."

Under most circumstances, the laws of the universe (and electricity) work in predictable ways. But since God is the Ruler of the world, He can suspend those rules whenever He chooses, to fit His own mysterious plans. Sondra has never doubted that. "But I am still astonished at the things God does," she says today, "not because He *can* do them, but because He would do them for me."[2]

The Thanksgiving Angel

*When you get into a tight place
and everything goes against you,
till it seems as though you could not
hang on a minute longer, never give
up then, for that is just the place
and time that the tide will turn.*

—HARRIET BEECHER STOWE

For many years, Ivy Olson privately pondered what came to be known as the Miracle, keeping it in a safe place in her heart. "I was afraid that if I shared it, people would say it was just a dream," she says. For what other explanation could there be?

But the event was real. Ivy never doubted it because it transformed not only the life she was leading at the time but her entire future. How could a mere illusion have such an effect?

Ivy grew up as the daughter of Seventh-Day Adventist missionaries. She spent her teens in a boarding school and went to nursing school in San Diego. Shortly after graduation, she married Michael, also a Seventh-Day Adventist. The sect was very strict, Ivy says. No dancing, no movies, no parties . . . the list went on. The young couple obeyed all the rules, shielding themselves as much as possible from what they regarded as the sinful world around them. But after the birth of their second son, Ivy became restless. Her life was so rigid, so restricted—just her work in a doctor's office and her duties at home. She longed for friends, for new experiences, for laughter and fun. "I tried to explain this to Michael, but he felt other people weren't to be trusted," Ivy recalls. Michael was furious when Ivy began bringing home books from the library that presented points of view about life different than their own. Yet she lacked the self-confidence to challenge him.

Then one day Ivy passed a movie theater which was playing a rerelease of *The Sound of Music*. She had never seen a movie. And how she longed to, especially one like this! She had heard that the story was inspiring, the music enough to move one to tears. "Can we go?" she asked Michael that evening.

He was horrified. "Absolutely not. You know the rules."

The rules. Ivy couldn't imagine a God so harsh that He would prohibit her the pleasure of music. For hadn't He created it?

So she went alone. "Sitting there in the theater, swept up in the experience, I faced the fact that I no longer believed in the faith of my youth," she says. But what to do? Leaving would open her up to ostracism by the entire religious community, even her parents. Yet staying would involve living a lie.

During the next several months, Ivy tried to share her new doubts with Michael, but he could not accept her questioning. Finally one day she packed up the boys and some possessions in her car. Perhaps if she got away for a while and thought things over . . . Michael followed her to the curb. "If you drive away now," he told her quietly, "don't ever come back."

Ivy looked at him. She wanted nothing more than to save her shaky marriage. But she had tried so hard to make herself into a person Michael—and the Church—would find acceptable. Obeying the rules and regulations. Hoping to be loved. Obviously, she had failed. With trembling fingers, she turned the ignition key and drove down the street.

"The first several months were extremely difficult," Ivy remembers. "I found a little apartment near the beach. It had one bedroom, but we had no furniture, so we all slept on the floor together." Michael occasionally sent money and visited the boys, but he didn't contest the divorce. Then he had an accident and was unable to make child support payments. Ivy's parents, away in the mission field and upset over her decision to leave Michael, offered no help. Everything—rent, food, and clothing—was now Ivy's responsibility.

Ivy's kind physician-boss was the only one who knew of her situation. Occasionally he "happened" to have an extra piece of furniture he thought she could use. But her financial struggle was exhausting. "By the time I paid day care and all the bills, the only place left to skimp was on food," she says. Yet how could she let her growing boys go hungry? Once Ivy applied for food stamps. But the clerk told her she earned two dollars above the cutoff point and wasn't eligible. She fled the welfare office, tears streaming down her cheeks.

Worse was her loneliness. How she longed for a friend, someone who might provide some interesting conversation or encouragement. For how was she going to handle this huge load? Was life ever going to be better? Would there be a time when she wasn't so frightened, so weary? Perhaps if she reached out, joined a group, even met some tenants in her build-ing . . . But her lifelong detachment from social situations had left scars. Who, she wondered, would be interested in knowing *her,* in seeing what a mess she had made of her life?

As Thanksgiving neared that year, life got even harder. No one was going to invite her and the boys for a holiday dinner, Ivy realized, because they had no friends who knew of their situation. On Thanksgiving morning she awakened, aware that she had only three hot dogs and three buns in the refrigerator. There was no money, and payday wasn't until the next week.

It was the lowest Ivy had been. "I put on a brave face—the same face I'd been wearing all this time—packed up the boys and the food, and went to the park. We laughed and played ball and ran barefoot through the grass and cooked our hot dogs on a grill." But as the trio walked home, one of the boys looked up at Ivy.

"I'm still hungry, Mom," he announced.

"Me too," his brother echoed. "Do we have anything else to eat?"

Ivy's heart sank. They were approaching the stairs to their apartment, and the weekend suddenly loomed very long and discouraging. What was she going to do?

Just then the door to basement apartment Number Three opened, and an elderly lady came out. "Oh, I'm glad I caught you, Ivy," she beamed. "I was going to ask you and the children to Thanksgiving dinner, but you were out when I knocked on your door earlier."

"Thanksgiving dinner?" Ivy's older son asked hopefully.

"Turkey and dressing and pumpkin pie . . ." The lady smiled at him.

"Mom! Can we?"

Ivy was staring at the little woman. Who was she? Ivy had never seen her before. True, her days were long and difficult, but shouldn't she recognize a neighbor who lived below, especially since the woman knew *her* name? Ivy's natural shyness rose. "I— Thank you, but . . ." She began to turn away.

"Oh, Mommy, please can't we have dinner here?" the younger boy begged. The aroma of roasting turkey wafted out the apartment door.

Ivy looked at her sons. How could she say no to them? "I have your favorite potato salad too, honey." The elderly lady smiled at Ivy. Her favorite . . . It seemed like years since she had tasted it. The scents and the warmth, but especially the neighbor's friendliness, touched her heart.

"Thank you," Ivy said quietly and followed her eager children into the apartment. It was nicely furnished, with soft welcoming light and a table beautifully set for four. The lady had planned on their company. How odd.

But dinner was ready, and almost in a daze Ivy sat down to the most wonderful meal she had had in years, perhaps ever. Turkey, yes, and stuffing, vegetables, soft rolls, that special potato salad. But most of all, love. The apartment seemed to be filled with it. It was as if they had dropped into a story, like the ones she often read to the boys, a make-believe scene full of joy and wonder, with their very own grandmother in charge of everything.

"This is marvelous," Ivy sighed contentedly as she buttered her third roll. "But I'm surprised I haven't seen you around, Miss . . . ?"

"Oh, I pop in and out." Their hostess beamed again. "How are you and the doctor getting along?"

"Very well," Ivy answered. "I like my job, but I do get lonely sometimes. Well, you live alone—you probably understand what it's like when no one's there." She could hardly believe she was talking so freely about things that had hurt her so deeply for so long.

"Oh, honey." The woman leaned closer. "I'm never alone, and neither are you."

"I'm not?" Ivy blinked.

"Of course not. And don't be afraid to ask for help—everyone needs it now and then. More stuffing, boys? No? Then how about dessert?"

They left the basement apartment weighted down with extra food. Ivy almost floated up the stairs. Filled with vigor, she was a completely different person than the forlorn woman of a few hours ago. She could do it, she knew. She could hold her little family together, no matter how difficult it might be. She was a "honey," someone special, someone worth talking to and caring about, and life held great promise for her. The lady—Ivy hadn't even gotten her name—had somehow shown her all of that and more.

The following morning Ivy bounced down the stairs and headed for Number Three. She had rooted a plant from her larger one to give to the lady. It wasn't much, but it was the only way Ivy could think of to say thank you. She knocked on the door.

No one answered. Ivy knocked again. Strange. It was so early. Where had the lady gone?

What if the woman was ill? Ivy stood on tiptoe and peeked through the window. What she saw sent tingles down her spine.

The apartment was vacant. No nice furniture, no lamps or rugs or even curtains, nothing but dust looking as if it hadn't been disturbed in months. Stunned, Ivy checked the apartment number. Yes, Number Three, the same door she and the boys had entered last night. But where was the little table, the homey touches? What had happened to the dishes and the food—and the wonderful lady?

The apartment manager lived on the same level, just around the corner. Ivy knocked on his door. "Apartment Number Three . . ." she asked as he opened the door. "Do you know the woman who lives there?"

The manager frowned. "Nobody lives there," he said.

"But my children and I had Thanksgiving dinner there yesterday . . ."

He shook his head. "Couldn't have. It's been empty for months."

Impossible. And yet hadn't there been clues all around her—her favorite potato salad, information about her employer, little things she should have noticed if she had wanted to question them? Ivy headed up the stairs, her mind racing. She had lived through a miracle. For a few hours, she had been graced with a love so intense, so wholesome and unconditional, that it could only have come from one Source. And she would never forget it.

Seven years later, Ivy's teenaged sons decided to live with their father. Although Ivy understood and accepted the move, she would miss them. On the other hand she would, for the first time, have some extra money. She decided to splurge on a plane ticket to Hawaii to visit a friend. There she met the pastor of a Lutheran church, fell in love, and married him. There she got involved in a variety of church ministries. In 1989, there was a building boom in Honolulu, and many families in the congregation, unable to pay their skyrocketing rents, suddenly became homeless. "I looked at them, at their bewilderment, confusion, and sense of hopelessness—and I saw myself years ago," Ivy says. She had never told anyone, not even her husband, about her experience that Thanksgiving Day. But one evening at a church board meeting, one of the members asked, "Before we adjourn, is there any new mission business?"

Ivy put up her hand. "I'd like to tell you all a story," she began.

Today Ivy is the director of the Angel Network, a self-help group for people in need in the Honolulu area. "We give them practical help," Ivy explains, "as well as the tools to become self-sufficient. We try to show them that someone is paying attention to them, that they are 'honeys,' even if that's hard to believe right now."

Angel Network has been a walk of faith, she says. But no one knows better than Ivy where the path began.[3]

Angels All around Us

Angels descending, bringing from
above,
Echoes of mercy, whispers of love.

—ANONYMOUS

Was it an angel who stepped in at the very moment Ivy Olson needed her most? Probably. And one of the most significant changes in society during the past few years is the almost wholesale acceptance of angels and the fact that they are indeed working in our world. Of course angels are often portrayed inaccurately in the media, as the spirits of those who have died, for example, or sweet cherubs come to play with us rather than members of the army of God, as Scripture has described them. "When you're talking about angels, you're talking about God," points out Martha Williamson, producer of the beloved *Touched by an Angel* television series. "And to most people, God means religion, and folks just don't trust television to treat religion with much respect. As a matter of fact, many letters our second year [on television] were from new converts to the show who had purposely avoided *Touched* the first season, because they were afraid of what Hollywood would do to angels."

But as the involvement of angels on earth continues, a growing number of people are willing to accept their presence, especially at times of catstrophe. During the aftermath of the tragic Oklahoma City bombing in April 1995, many people claimed to see angels hovering over the building, or standing in front of it, wings outstretched. And when USAir Flight 427 had gone down in September 1994, several children playing soccer in a field insisted that when they looked up to see the plane, most of them saw angels flying around it.

But an angel's job is not always to "carry us home." Sometimes they are sent to protect us or our loved ones. And "sometimes you don't even *know* you need help," Rhonda Christie points out.

For example, several summers ago, while living in Mobile, Alabama, Rhonda and her husband, John, carefully tucked their two-year-old daughter Kellie into bed each night, then conscientiously checked her again before they went to sleep. Kellie had developed a habit of dragging a tiny red rocking chair around with her, which both John and Rhonda would often trip over. "No," Rhonda would laugh, "you can't take the chair to bed with you!" But they would put it as close to Kellie's bed as they could.

One night they followed the usual routine and were awakened hours later by the insistent ringing of the doorbell. John bolted out of bed. "Who could that be?" he muttered, glancing at the clock. It was almost 2:00 A.M.

Rhonda, curious and concerned, followed John to the front door, watching as he flung it open. A young man in cutoff jeans and a white T-shirt stood there, a bike propped up behind him. In his arms was their pajama-clad daughter, Kellie! Incredibly, she was holding her favorite doll and her little red rocking chair.

It couldn't be! Kellie had been sleeping soundly the last time they checked. How had she ended up outside, in the middle of the night, with this stranger? "I think I must have freaked out for a moment," Rhonda recalls. "I couldn't believe what I was seeing."

John was equally shocked. "Where did you get her?" he asked, grabbing his daughter out of the young man's arms.

"I found her walking down Main Street, carrying her doll and that little red rocker," the stranger said calmly.

Rhonda gasped. Main Street was almost two miles from their subdivision, a very busy and dangerous area. Kellie could have been hit by a car or injured or . . . Rhonda couldn't bear to think about it. She looked more closely at the young man. He was beautiful, she realized, with curly blond hair and eyes that seemed to look right into her soul.

John wanted more details. He turned for a moment and placed Kellie in Rhonda's arms. But when they turned back to question the young man, he was gone.

"Our street was long and straight, and we should have been able to see him riding down our driveway or on the street on his bike," Rhonda says. "But although we went outside to look, we saw nothing at all." During those few distracted seconds, the stranger had vanished. Rhonda and John spent the rest of the night giving thanks to God for bringing their daughter safely home to them.

It was only later that another question occurred to them. Kellie didn't speak very distinctly at that age and certainly didn't know her address or telephone number. How had the young man known where to bring her?

"This ten- or fifteen-second encounter left its mark on our family," Rhonda says today. "I know that angels are real."

Anthony Coda had joined the navy and was serving on a cargo ship, the USS *Ariel*. The crew took ammunition to Iceland and Newfoundland and brought troops and supplies back to the States. One beautiful day, the *Ariel* was anchored off Chesapeake Bay, and most of the crew was on leave. It wasn't Anthony's turn to leave the ship, and he was restless. He paced back and forth on the empty deck, wishing someone was around to talk to. Finally, he decided to go for a swim. "I went to the well deck and jumped in the ocean," he says. "I'm not a strong swimmer, and I'm slow, but I do like being in the water."

Anthony had intended to stay right next to the ship. But he felt the ocean current giving him a push. Faster and faster, Anthony let the current carry him along for ten or fifteen minutes. The ride was exhilarating. But when Anthony finally turned around, his heart sank. He had gone much too far from the ship. "The *Ariel* was the size of a matchbook," he says. "I knew I could never swim back—especially not against the tide."

But he tried. Stroke after stroke. But still he was no match for the ocean current that was flowing in the opposite direction. Each time he gained some ground and paused for a moment to rest his now-aching arms and legs, the tide would push him back again. The *Ariel* seemed even farther away.

"Help!" Anthony shouted. But his words blew away in the strong wind. For the first time he sank underwater, then thrust himself up, his lungs bursting. "Help—I'm drowning!" Again he shouted. But there was no one to hear him.

Anthony's arms and legs were heavy as logs, and he knew he was going to die. Once again, he dipped under the waves and surfaced for what would surely be the last time. He thought of his loved ones, who would never understand why this had happened to him. "God," he prayed, tears mingling with the salty water on his face, "please help me." Again he sank under the waves. It was the last thing he remembered. . . .

He woke up on the well deck, lying in a pool of water, soaked and exhausted, but apparently unharmed. No one was on deck but Anthony. Everything around him was as quiet and deserted as it had been before he jumped into the bay.

Did an angel pull him out of the water and deposit him safely back at his post? "I never knew what happened," he says. Except that, with God, nothing is impossible.

Mayre Lou Montessoro had to drop her car off at the auto repair shop one morning, so her husband, Paul, drove her to the tiny jewelry shop where she worked. She was enjoying living on Guam and learning all she could about buying and selling gold jewelry from Thailand. "But the store is so vulnerable," she told Paul once again as they rode along. "We're way out in the boonies. The phone doesn't work there, so of course the burglar alarm doesn't, either. I keep feeling like we're going to be robbed at any minute." Mayre Lou's faith had always been strong, and that morning she had prayed for protection for all the store workers, feeling the urge to read Psalm 91. "I had never read it before," she says, "and didn't know what the word 'pinions' meant." But it had made her feel a little better, as if God were reassuring her in some way.

Paul tried to console her. "If anyone did try to hold you up, all they'd want would be the jewelry and money," he pointed out. "If you just gave them everything, they wouldn't hurt you."

"I suppose you're right," Mayre Lou admitted.

When they reached the store, Carol, the owner, was there alone, her husband having been delayed in Hong Kong due to a storm. Mayre Lou began to feel vulnerable again. Just two women in the store today . . . She and Paul shared their concerns with Carol. "Sometimes I feel like that too," Carol confessed. "But if we're ever robbed, just hand everything over. I'm sure we'd be safe then."

Paul left and Carol opened the store. For the first few hours the store was very busy. Then everything quieted down, with just one woman customer browsing.

Suddenly two men plunged through the front door, wearing children's Halloween masks and waving rifles. Mayre Lou was stunned. For a moment she thought it was someone's idea of a horrible joke, that the guns must be toys.

But when one of the men tossed a paper bag at her and mumbled something that she couldn't understand, she found her voice. "What do you want?" she asked shakily.

The men seemed terribly nervous, but Carol reached for the cash box. "Here." She shoved it toward them. "Take all the money."

Just then the other man, who had been moving about aimlessly, struck the female customer on the head with the butt of his rifle. As Mayre Lou watched the woman slip silently to the floor, she realized fully how much danger they were in. "Everything seemed to be in slow motion, as if our brains were rejecting the reality of it all," she says. "It wasn't real. It couldn't be." Things like this didn't happen to ordinary people like Carol and her.

The man who had thrown the bag at Mayre Lou waved his rifle and shouted at her. She couldn't understand him and didn't know how to respond—which seemed to make him even angrier. Suddenly he aimed the rifle at her stomach. *Click. Click.* Frantically, he pumped the rifle's loading device, ejecting empty shells, but the gun wouldn't fire. *If only I could faint now and wake up when this is all over,* Mayre Lou thought. Surely a bullet would hit her at any moment.

But nothing did. The women and two more customers who had wandered unsuspectingly into the shop were all pushed to the floor. They hid their faces in their hands while the robbers grabbed all the gold necklaces from the cases. The man with the rifle kept it pointed at Mayre Lou's head the entire time but didn't attempt to fire it again. Finally, after stuffing the paper bags with cash, the men took the customers' purses and ran out the front door without a word to anyone inside. "We expected they would make a noisy exit or warn us to be quiet but we heard nothing at all," Mayre Lou recalls. "I remember thinking I would lie there all day if I had to, just to be sure they were gone." But finally, as quiet minutes passed and her pounding heart began to return to a normal pace, Mayre Lou lifted her head slightly and realized that she, Carol, and the customers were alone in the store. Slowly, numbly, they began to stand up. "Are you all right?" they asked one another.

A gentleman dashed into the store with a description of the getaway car. Carol went to the police station, since the phone wasn't working. The customers were shaky; two wept and the one who had been hit on the head was eventually taken to the hospital.

And one lady pointed to something on the floor in front of the case where Mayre Lou had been standing. It was a .22-caliber bullet casing.

"The realization that he really had tried to shoot me suddenly made my head reel," Mayre Lou says. "That thought still refuses to leave my mind." When she showed the casing to the police, they simply shook their heads. "Lucky lady," they murmured. Why had the gun malfunctioned at that precise moment? Or, if it was in good working order, how—aiming point-blank at her twice—could the man have missed?

The robbers were caught some forty-five minutes later, Carol has closed the store, and slowly everyone is healing from this frightening ordeal. And Mayre Lou finds special significance in the fact that she prayed Psalm 91 that morning. *Pinions,* she has since discovered, refers to wing tips. Was her life spared by the wings of invisible angels, circling her in protection? Perhaps she'll never know. But she is grateful for each new day and each opportunity to learn more about these heavenly guardians.

Touches from Above

> They that love beyond the world
> cannot be separated by it . . . they
> live in one another still.
>
> —WILLIAM PENN
>
> FRUITS OF SOLITUDE

Gifts of love and comfort are probably not limited to angels. For wouldn't this glorious Creator, knowing how much we mourn for those who have gone ahead to heaven, allow them to cross that spiritual boundary occasionally to minister to us?

Swish, thump. Swish, thump. Floriana Hall rocked back and forth on the wooden floor, feeding her newborn granddaughter, Nikki, in the old rocker and wondering idly how many bottles she had fed to babies during her life. The new parents—Floriana's daughter Joyce and son-in-law Ed—were living with Floriana's family temporarily and everything was going well. Except for this middle-of-the-night feeding, which was awfully difficult for Floriana, even though she wanted to give Joyce a break once in a while. No wonder God gave babies to younger women!

Swish, thump. The rocker went on with its steady beat. Floriana's thoughts turned to her own mother, who had died suddenly not that long ago. Floriana still remembered how shocked she had been upon hearing the news. Her mother, only fifty-nine years old; Floriana, with five children yet to grow up and have their own families—her mother would miss all that! Floriana couldn't stop weeping about it.

Then one night in a dream her mother had come to her. "Floriana," she had said, "I want you to go on with your life. I'm fine and happy."

It was a turning point for Floriana. She had stopped mourning after a time, and gotten back to her usual chores and schedules. And now here was this baby filling their home with new life! It was a delightful time, and even though Floriana was enjoying it, she occasionally found herself thinking about her own mother. How she wished for a small sign, anything to let her know that Mom was watching over them from heaven and knew about Nikki.

Swish, thump. Swish, thump . . . Little Nikki had fallen asleep, so Floriana carefully carried her into the spare bedroom and put her down. Nikki was a good baby except when she would go on a crying jag sometimes at night. The house wasn't very big, so when Nikki was awake, Floriana and Joyce were too. The men, however, seemed to be able to sleep through anything. They always claimed, the morning after, that they had never heard the baby. The women didn't know whether to believe them or not.

"I think the baby's getting ready to stop that middle-of-the-night feeding," Joyce remarked to Floriana a few days later as they prepared breakfast. "She slept through until past four this morning."

No wonder Floriana hadn't heard anything. She hated to admit how grateful she would be when she could sleep an uninterrupted night. Even though Joyce usually got up with Nikki, Floriana always awakened too.

The following night Floriana was in a deep sleep when she heard Nikki's little whimper. She squinted at the clock. Two o'clock. No, Nikki was old enough now to go back to sleep. She didn't actually *need* this feeding. *Babies have to be disciplined too,* Floriana told herself as she listened to see if Nikki was going to be cooperative. It didn't sound like it.

Well . . . she sighed. Joyce had taken the feeding the past few nights. Maybe Floriana should get up. Slowly she swung herself up to a sitting position, reached for her robe, and . . .

Swish, thump. Swish, thump. It was the welcome sound of the rocker. How could Joyce have warmed the bottle so quickly? But Floriana wasn't about to argue. *Swish, thump.* It sounded like everything was already under control.

Gratefully, Floriana snuggled back under the blankets.

The following morning Floriana was cooking breakfast when Joyce came into the kitchen. She put her arm around Floriana and gave her a big hug. "Mom, thanks. You're a doll."

"For what?" Floriana continued scrambling eggs.

"For getting up last night with Nikki so I could sleep. It felt so good."

"What are you talking about?" Floriana turned the stove off as her husband and son-in-law came into the kitchen. "I didn't get up last night."

"Sure you did. I heard the rocking chair."

"Maybe she just stopped crying and went back to sleep," Floriana suggested. "You know she did that once before." But Floriana had heard the *swish, thump* of the rocking chair too.

The men were astonished. "I hardly ever hear anything," Ed admitted, "but last night I heard the chair too. It went on and on—I remember wondering if you were going to rock the baby until dawn."

Joyce and Floriana never found an empty bottle, nor did Nikki end her night feedings immediately after that. But Floriana never again wondered if her mother was aware of what was going on in the family. Mom would "be there" for all the special events that still awaited them. Floriana knew that now for sure.

People of all nationalities and religious faiths have heard of Padre Pio, the Capuchin priest from San Giovanni Rotondo, Italy, who bore the stigmata—the wounds of Christ—for the last fifty years of his life. (During his frequent medical examinations, many doctors confirmed that the holes were so large that one could almost see through them, from one side of Padre Pio's hand to the other.) He died in September 1968, and the Catholic Church is considering canonizing him—that is, making him an "official" saint of the Church. During Padre Pio's life, he exhibited many examples of phenomena—there was often an aroma of strong perfume announcing his presence, and he could read people's souls to determine whether or not they were telling the truth. His prophecies and miraculous cures were witnessed by thousands. Padre Pio also had the gift of bilocation—being seen in two places at the same time. Far from ending now that he is home in heaven, Padre Pio seems to be still using his gifts to help those on earth who ask him.

Recently, Doris H., who is a devout woman and well-known to the staff of *The Padre Pio Gazette* in Middletown, Connecticut, e-mailed a request for prayers for a friend of hers, Dorothy. Dorothy was fighting cancer, and another tumor had appeared on her arm. Her physician had told her earlier that if the cancer was spreading, he would not operate on her anymore.

"I went to mass on August 12 and knelt next to Dorothy," Doris told the staff at the *Gazette*. "Dorothy asked if I would pray that she would be healed. Of course I said yes." While Doris was kneeling, she saw a bearded man approach. "When he came closer, I could see a golden light around him, and he smiled at me," she says. Doris recognized him from the many photos she had seen: It was Padre Pio!

Doris was not afraid. Instead, she asked this saintly man if he would help Dorothy.

"Yes," Padre Pio said. "Tell her to pray to Jesus for three days. But she must have faith and show that faith. There is faith . . . and there is *true* faith. It is the true faith that counts."

Not everyone who prays for a healing, even with true faith, will receive it, Padre Pio told Doris. But they will all find peace. Then the saintly priest's image faded. Doris immediately gave the Padre's message to Dorothy, who was overjoyed.

On August 15, Dorothy was scheduled for tests. First, she attended early mass, where Doris caught sight of her kneeling in a pew. "After mass, I went outside to talk to her, but I was too late—she was already in her car, backing up," Doris says. There was a man sitting next to her in the car. Doris assumed it was Dorothy's husband.

"But when the car changed direction, I saw the man's face. He had a beard, and her husband does not." The man turned around, looked directly at Doris, smiled at her, and put his hand up. It was Padre Pio again!

Doris was flooded with peace, love, and—most of all—confidence for her friend. "When he said he would be with Dorothy in the hospital, I believed him," Doris explains. But she had been shocked to see just *how* close this wonderful man was planning to be.

Padre Pio was as good as his word. Dorothy came home the very same day. "The doctors were amazed—the cancer has not spread, and they said I'm going to completely recover," she told Doris.

Doris was not surprised. She and Dorothy both thank the Padre every day for the gifts he has given.[4]

Susan Gibson, a first-grade teacher from Enola, Pennsylvania, had been hospitalized for a severe allergic reaction, which left her frightened. "After that, I started to live my life a bit differently," she says. Susan had once been a member of a church and sung in its choir. Because her grandmother and aunt still attended that church (and her grandmother kept making pointed remarks on how nice it would be if she came back), Susan decided to go with them one Sunday morning.

"As we walked into the church, which was rather crowded, I saw two friends of mine—Gail and her husband, Walt—who I'd used to sing with in choir," Susan recalls. "Gail was standing right behind Walt, leaning over his shoulder with her hymnal in her hand and her robe on. They both have beautiful voices and I had always wanted Gail to sing at my wedding." Susan decided she would have to go and give them both a hug. But by the time she worked her way through the crowd, she found only Walt. He was obviously happy to see her after so much time, and they chatted briefly, but soon the chimes rang, announcing the beginning of services. Susan went up one aisle and down the other, back to her pew, sticking her head in the choir loft to wave at Gail and wish her good luck.

But Gail wasn't in the loft, and as the service began and the choir sang the first song, Susan realized that Gail didn't seem to be anywhere in the choir. Walt was in his usual place; Gail usually stood right next to him. But today there was no sign of her. And yet Susan was absolutely certain she had seen her old friend; it had not been someone else. Had Gail suddenly gotten sick and left?

Susan had been holding the church bulletin, and now she flipped through it. On the second page, she noticed the IN MEMORY section. Toward the bottom was Gail's name, under the heading, IN LOVING MEMORY OF MY WIFE, FROM WALT.

Susan started to giggle. Gail would be furious at Walt's mistake. Or maybe it was a practical joke. "Gram," she whispered. "Look— Walt put Gail's name in the memorials instead of the dedication column."

Susan's grandmother gave her a peculiar look.

"Speaking of Gail, where *is* she?" Susan murmured to her aunt. "I saw her a little earlier, but . . ."

Susan's aunt pulled a pencil out of her purse and took Susan's bulletin. Down at the bottom, near the memorials, she wrote, "You couldn't have seen her earlier. Gail is dead. She died a few months ago."

Susan read the scribble, stunned. She couldn't believe it. How could Gail have died without her hearing about it? Why had she not been informed of the funeral or somehow gotten involved in the mourning?

It was because she had chosen not to be a part of the church community, she knew. She wouldn't let that happen again.

"My grandmother and aunt eventually believed that I *had* seen Gail, because I was so positive about it," Susan says. "No halos, wings, or bright lights. Just Gail. Maybe she was letting me know that she and her music would always be nearby and that she was happy in her new life. It was a moment I'll never forget."

After giving a talk in a bookstore in Indiana, I asked if anyone in the audience had a story to share. A young man named Mike told of a time when he was about ten and was allowed to stay home to watch Saturday-morning cartoons on television while his parents and younger sister went grocery shopping.

"My grandparents lived about forty miles away, and on Saturdays, Grandpa often came over about eleven," Mike recalls. "Sometimes he'd be dressed in his old clothes, which meant that he was going to help my dad with maintenance around the house. But sometimes he'd be wearing something new. I always knew *that* meant that he and I were going out to lunch, just by ourselves."

Mike loved his grandpa and was delighted, one particular Saturday morning, to hear the key in the kitchen door. He turned around and saw Grandpa coming in wearing a new green plaid shirt. Yes! It was lunch, for him and Grandpa. He waved to Grandpa, and Grandpa waved back, then blew Mike a kiss, as was his custom. Mike turned back to the television to watch the last of a cartoon.

A minute or two later, he switched off the set and went into the kitchen to ask Grandpa about the details of the day. But the kitchen was empty. Had Grandpa gone down to the basement? Mike scrambled down the stairs, but everything was dark. When he came up he went outside, just in time to see his family pulling into the driveway. "Grandpa was here," Mike told his father. "But I don't see him now."

"Well, he has to be somewhere, maybe talking to the neighbors?" Mike and his father began to hunt for him. Grandpa was nowhere to be found.

Puzzled, they came into the kitchen just as the phone rang. Mike's father answered it. Slowly his face turned pale. "I'll be over right away, Mom," he told her, then hung up and turned to his family. "That was Grandma," he said. "She's home, and she just went into the living room, where Grandpa had been reading the paper, and found him . . . dead."

Dead! "But . . ." Mike began.

"He had planned to leave in just a few minutes to drive over here to take you out to lunch, Mike," Dad went on, his eyes filling up. "His heart just stopped."

"Did Grandma say what he was wearing?" Mike asked.

"Yes, she did. A new green plaid shirt."

Now, some fifteen years later, Mike says that this incident never scared him or made him feel spooked. "I feel today just as I felt that morning," he says. "I thought it was great of God to let my grandpa stop by on his way to heaven and blow me one last kiss."

Mississippi Miracle

*Then the glory of God shall be
revealed,
And all humankind shall see it
together.*

—ISAIAH 40:5

To most of us, rain is just a part of nature, something that nurtures our flower gardens or makes driving more difficult. But rain evokes many biblical symbols as well. As we recall, God once sent a forty-day flood to wipe out the population and start the world all over again because His people had turned against His commandments.

Mary Talken wasn't thinking of anything quite so lofty when, on St. Patrick's Day 1993, she looked out her kitchen window and noticed that it was raining. She lives on the bluffs that overlook the Mississippi River in Quincy, Illinois, and there were still seven inches of snow on the ground. Farmers were beginning to watch the small rivers and lakes with some concern.

Showers continued almost every day during the remainder of March, in addition to a two-foot snowfall in Sioux City, Iowa, and a ten-foot-high ice jam in Minnesota, all of which would have to melt and travel south past Quincy. The townspeople were becoming concerned. "During April, Quincy had hit-or-miss rainfall, with the river depth rising and going down again slightly but always between seventeen and twenty-one feet," Mary says. "Still, normal depth is around eleven feet, with flood stage about seventeen feet, so people started sandbagging just to be on the safe side." Hannibal, Missouri, a city south of Quincy on the river, installed a new flood system. Up north some residents evacuated their homes. But, as one native put it, "If you don't like water, you oughtn't live here."

Looking ahead, experts forecast a twenty-one-foot crest, definitely manageable. No one yet knew that a flood of over thirty-one feet—which had a one in five hundred chance of happening in any given year—was on its way.

The disaster started slowly, ominously. In mid-April, a creek overflowed its banks and reached to the edges of homes. Businesses in several riverfront cities were surrounded by water, and a leak was discovered in one of the levees. "It was muddy but calm," Mary recalls. "People cleaned up the silt from the riverfront parks and assumed the worst was over."

But the rain kept falling onto the already-saturated ground, making the river current flow twice as fast as usual, causing barges to crash into one another and—once again—raising the river. On June 30, the first levee broke, initially flooding eight hundred acres. That night lightning and thunder shook houses, high winds blew over power lines, and six inches of rain poured into basements. The river flowed south at five times its normal speed, breaking height records wherever it went.

Fortunately for Mary and most of Quincy's 40,000-plus residents, their houses were spared because the city is located high on a rocky hill that follows the winding river for many miles. But some of Mary's friends in low-lying areas were not so fortunate.

By now the flood was national news, and the hearts of many around the country ached for those directly affected by it. Quincyans began round-the-clock sandbagging, the elderly sitting in lawn chairs, holding bags open while younger people filled them. Others worked the riverbank itself, adding bags to any weak spots they found. Quincy's mayor mobilized inmates from the county jail to help. Locks and dams were closed to let the river flow freely, but this stranded hundreds of boats and caused a traffic nightmare. People flocked to vantage points along the bluff to view the ever-rising water, as others continued to evacuate.

"We're going to win this battle," Mary told a group of neighbors who met one day. "We've been praying, haven't we?" The media had been great too, staying available round the clock, getting messages from people on the levee to those who could bring insect repellent, sunscreen, hats, dry socks—whatever was needed.

"It looks hopeful," said one of the women, watching the National Guard patrol while nurses gave tetanus shots and the Salvation Army, Red Cross, and people from out of town brought food and found lodging for the growing number of evacuees.

"But . . ." a third reminded them, looking up at the sky, "it's still raining."

On July 8, another levee broke. Floodwaters inundated thousands upon thousands of acres of farmland downriver, and angry waters lapped at the roofs of houses. Exhausted residents watched, tears streaming down their cheeks. "We're going down like dominos," one woman sobbed. By now the Mississippi was at an all-time unbelievable high of thirty-two feet, and homes were actually being washed away. Would towns like West Quincy and those lower areas still dry be saved?

No. On Friday evening, July 16, at 8:22 P.M.,

the West Quincy levee broke, sucking two barges through the opening, rupturing the gas tanks of a flooded service station, and causing a huge fire that fed on the gasoline that now spread across the river. What everyone feared most had happened: The Quincy bridges were now closed; there was no way to cross the Mississippi from St. Louis all the way north to the Quad-Cities (Moline/Rock Island/Davenport/Bettendorf) for the foreseeable future.

The newly elected mayor was both exhausted and confounded. What more could he—or anyone—do? Then gradually an idea began to grow. Yes, the people had been praying in their own hearts and churches, but why not hold a public prayer service? Obviously, God could help them. He should be acknowledged openly.

Hundreds of residents attended the prayer service, held the following day in City Hall's parking lot. Clergy of varying faiths led the group in heartfelt prayer and beautiful hymns of praise. "We acknowledged God as the Creator of all things and asked Him to come to our aid and save what was left to be saved," Mary says. Neighbor next to neighbor, all faiths, united in a common cause as perhaps, aeons ago, they were meant to be . . . Everyone went home with a small sense of comfort. Now they had done *everything* they could.

The rain did not stop. In fact, a few days later, another storm hit the area. But oddly, the river's depth began to drop, never again reaching thirty-two feet. By the end of August, despite still-continuous showers, the Mississippi had inexplicably dwindled to twenty-three feet, and people were beginning to attack the twelve-billion-plus dollars in damage that had been left by the flood of '93.

Did the river stop rising because the people *publicly* acknowledged God's power and asked Him to take control? Or was it just a wonderful coincidence that the situation began to heal after people of many faiths prayed as a community? Were there more important things that God wanted to accomplish in Quincy, things that could only happen if the flood continued for a while? "I think the 'miracle' of the '93 flood was in the coming together of thousands of individuals," Mary says. "When times are good, everyone tends to their own lives, so if God had stopped the rain in early June, we probably would have mopped up the mud and moved on in our own little worlds. But perhaps the Lord allows natural disasters to occur so we'll turn our attention to Him, and to those in need."

Could Mary be right? One person who would probably agree with her is Sister Maurella Schlise, who brought the cookies to the prison on Christmas Eve. "Just to let you know," she wrote to me soon after the destructive Midwest flooding that occurred in spring 1997, "that almost our entire city of Fargo was spared the flood. Praise God! As I wrote to our newspaper editor, I believe it was because we have days and nights of prayer and adoration in our Catholic churches here.

"Nothing like this occurs in Grand Forks. Was it just a coincidence that about twelve thousand of the Grand Forks residents had to come and stay with us for a while while their city was being rebuilt?"

What Now, God?

*There's always an up- and a
downside to suffering, depending on
what you do with it.*

—DR. LAURA SCHLESSINGER
ABC RADIO TALK SHOW HOST

When we realize how much God loves us
and how closely He watches over us,
we're apt to assume that nothing really bad will
ever happen to God's children, that we are protected in a special way, immune to the problems
of life. Nothing could be farther from the truth.
From such biblical characters as Job to present-

day disciples grappling with sickness or difficult decisions, everyone suffers. And while we're going through hardships, we may not always see the whole pattern or understand why. Yet, somehow, God can make His glory shine through every circumstance.

Up until September of 1994, for example, Sheila Dawes★ was living what she considered to be a happy, settled life. Married, she was raising a three-year-old daughter. Then her grand-mother died after a long illness. "That was my first real loss in quite a while," Sheila says, "but I had no idea how much of my life was about to change."

About three weeks later, Sheila's mother-in-law died very suddenly. "She simply fell asleep on her couch and never woke up," Sheila remembers. It was quite a shock for everyone, especially Sheila's husband, Brad★. Brad was the youngest of his siblings, and he took his mother's death extremely hard. "His mother had always been there to catch him when he fell or to pick up the pieces," Sheila says. "I guess he felt he no longer had a safety net." Brad began to suffer from depression, which got worse by the week. Soon he could no longer work and completely broke down.

For the next several months, Brad was in and out of mental hospitals, taking a variety of medications and seeing counselors. Sheila did her best to shield their three-year-old from the answers to her constant questions—"Where is Daddy? Why is he sick?" and to give Brad the support he needed. The bills were beginning to mount, and the stress was terrible. There were plenty of sleepless nights when Sheila tossed and turned. She had a very sick husband. Was he going to recover, or was he doomed to a lifetime of mental institutions? Where was the money going to come from? How would Sheila raise her child alone? What had she done to deserve this? Where was God? "But each time I began to lose it, for some reason, I'd suddenly regain my strength and be able to continue on. We have a wonderful family and great friends who were there for both of us throughout this time." Someone would bring a dinner or a card or a hug. An answer—or an insight—would come. Sheila would sense, somehow, that someone was praying intensely for her, and it would provide her with just the right amount of energy to take another step. She learned to live—and pray—one day at a time. Not because she was a hero, she'd explain, but because there really was no alternative.

At the end of January 1995, Sheila's uncle died of cancer. Sheila drove her mother to his house that morning, then went on to work. It was about an hour away on a busy expressway. "About fifteen minutes from the office, my van began to make a funny noise," she recalls. "I remember talking out loud to the car, tapping the dashboard as if I could actually persuade it to keep on going. As smoke started pouring from the back, I got scared and pulled off."

Immediately a white truck pulled up in front of her. Now Sheila was even more frightened. Not only was she stuck, but there were two strange men coming toward her. There were always stories in the local newspapers about this kind of thing. She started to pray.

As she looked at them, she realized that they were waving at her to get out of the van. "It's on fire!" one shouted.

She'd had no idea! As she jumped from the van, she realized that one of the men had a fire extinguisher, and he quickly put out the fire. The other told her that a tow truck would be arriving soon, and they would wait with her until it came. "Although the exits on this expressway are few and far between, and I never saw either of the men use a cell phone, a tow truck did indeed pull up about five minutes later," Sheila says. "The two men simply returned to their car and drove off. I never got their names nor can I remember what they looked like.

"To add to the blessing, the tow truck driver took me straight to my office, despite the dispatcher's telling him his truck was needed back at the shop. These men may not have been heavenly angels, but I do believe God was watching over me during this entire time of trouble. He knew I was close to the breaking point and would need all my energy for the months ahead."

By early April, Brad was scheduled to be released from the hospital. He had been a patient this last stay for about four weeks. Sheila was happy about him coming home but apprehensive, too. Brad was frequently incoherent, because his medication had not been regulated properly yet, and Sheila worried about whether she could manage everything. Then disaster struck again. "The night before his release, while I was answering the front door, I slipped, fell, and broke my ankle severely in three places. I was taken to the hospital, had surgery, and was told I would have to stay there a whole week," Sheila recalls.

At first she was panic-stricken—what would happen now? *God,* she prayed. *Why are you allowing all this to happen to me? I feel so abandoned.* She had looked forward so long to Brad's return, and now she would not be there to greet him.

Sheila's parents took her daughter, and Brad's family stepped in once again, reassuring Sheila that they would look after Brad until she was out of the hospital, and more steady on her feet.

During the next few weeks, Sheila saw Brad only a few times. Each visit left her in tears, for he seemed no better. "I could not believe I had lost the only man I had ever loved—we met when we were sixteen. And worse, that our child might never get to know what a wonderful father she had!"

Then, like a resurrection, on Good Friday Brad's medications seemed to start working themselves out. Sheila answered the phone at her mother's house, where she had been staying after her release from the hospital, to hear Brad's voice, sounding the same as it always had. "I'm picking you up this afternoon, honey," he told her. "We're going home, and I'm going to take care of you myself. I called my boss, and I'm going back to work on Monday. Make a list of stuff we need for Easter."

Sheila wept again, this time tears of joy. After being so dependent for so long, Brad wanted to get back to his real life and move on. Sheila had feared this day would never come.

Slowly, as she and Brad renewed their life together, Sheila began to look back and see the wisdom of God's plan for her in this most recent seeming-catastrophe, the broken ankle. Perhaps she had not been ready to accept full responsibility for Brad when he was not as stable as he needed to be. Because she had become temporarily incapacitated, other people had to step in and help her.

And yet, why did *any* of this have to happen? This is the mystery of suffering, which we will not fully understand until we meet God face-to-face. And perhaps God's children will continue to be called upon to go through difficult times, in reparation for the sins of others or to help increase one another's faith. We really don't know why.

Yet "while those eight months were the most difficult we have ever experienced, I can say that we are much stronger for having gone through them," says Sheila. "We are all very grateful to be a family again. And I know God was watching over us through those rough times, just as He always does, and it was through His love that we survived."

Wrapped in Protection

Say to those whose hearts are
    frightened, "Be strong! Fear not!
Here is your God.
He comes with vindication, with
    divine recompense.
He comes to save you."

                     —*ISAIAH 35:4*

Why had he agreed to do this? Joe Weikel wondered, as he stood in the customs line at the border of Communist China, waiting for permission to enter. He was a middle-aged government worker on leave from his job in Washington, D.C.; why had he put himself in danger by taking this missions trip?

It was only a matter of minutes, he was

belatedly realizing, until he would be caught, pulled out of line, arrested, and sent to jail, possibly for years. For in his innocent-looking backpack, he was carrying fifty small Bibles written in Chinese—contraband strictly forbidden in this anti-Christian country. When the guard discovered them, anything could happen.

Furtively, Joe looked around for a route of escape. But there was none available. He was in a no-man's-land of urban congestion, consisting mostly of concrete and barbed wire between the bright, modern buildings of the Hong Kong New Territories and the dingy warehouses of Communist Shenzen. Surrounding him were lines of people waiting to be checked through; to bolt now would signal to everyone that he had something to hide. Perhaps his ten traveling companions, also carrying Bibles in their backpacks, would be arrested too, even though they seemed to have breezed through customs and were now waiting for him.

Inadvertently, Joe had chosen the slowest-moving line. This inspector was zealously checking every piece of luggage before stamping tourists' visas and passports. There was no way the Bibles would go unnoticed. Was his life of freedom coming to an end? *Help me, Lord* he prayed.

The whole episode had started in such an innocent way. Joe had taken a yearlong sabbatical from his government job to attend Fuller Theological Seminary in Pasadena, California, to prepare for a possible career in the ministry. The seminary offered six hours of graduate credit for a five-week mission trip; it involved two weeks studying in Hong Kong, two weeks touring mainland China, and a final week in Taiwan. The trip had sounded fascinating.

"In Hong Kong, before we left on our actual trip, we were required to complete a course on the persecution of the Chinese Christian Church," Joe explains. During the 1950s, he learned, missionaries were either expelled or jailed in China, and church services were held underground, usually in private homes. By the 1960s, government officials had confiscated almost every Bible in the country. Scriptures found their way into China through outside sources, but deliveries were risky because of the strict penalties imposed on anyone caught smuggling. "Right now, hundreds of Bibles are stacked up in this very church in Hong Kong in which you are preparing for your trip," church officials explained. "We are asking everyone, but especially college students, to smuggle in a few at a time, for persecuted Christians longing for the word of God."

"Isn't it dangerous to do this sort of thing?" Joe had asked, looking for a way out. After all, he was just here to complete requirements for a course, not to become a hero.

"Don't worry. You won't be caught. Guards don't check students with backpacks," church officials had assured him. "They're more interested in jewelry and drugs. Smuggling a few Bibles will be easy, especially for an older seminarian like you."

However, Joe had ended up swinging a backpack onto his shoulders that contained fifty Bibles—more than just "a few." The pack weighed seventy pounds once his clothing was added. And Joe had a history of back problems.

Furthermore, as Joe continued to stand in the customs line, the guard only inches away from him was turning over every item in the suitcase of the man ahead. *God, I didn't expect this,* Joe prayed silently, his heart pounding. *Please don't let me go to jail.*

And, just as silently, came a small whisper: *My grace is sufficient for you.*

Yes. It was. Joe had known that for nine years, ever since he had begun his walk with the Lord. God would never abandon or forsake him. Joe knew that the apostle Paul had gone to jail for his faith and that the Lord had been there to sustain him. That had happened with countless others, down through the centuries. If Joe *was* to end up in a Chinese jail because he had tried to spread the word of God, then the Lord would be there with him, too.

The knowledge, however, didn't still his fear. And the guard was so close now that Joe could smell his breath, fouled by bad teeth. Joe's arms felt so stiff that he could not reach up and remove the heavy backpack. Would the customs agent rip it from his shoulders and throw it to the cracked pavement? Would the Bibles spill out onto the ground, for everyone to see? Would Joe be led away in handcuffs?

The man in front of him had moved

through the turnstile toward the waiting train to Canton. Joe stepped forward, his hands out, ready to be grabbed and cuffed by the guard. "Next!" the guard barked in English. But not to Joe. To the man *behind* him, who had not stepped forward. Passing Joe as if he was not even there, the guard beckoned to this next man, his uniformed arm so close to Joe's face that Joe could feel the coarse gray material brush his cheek. "Step forward! Open your suitcases!" he yelled to the man behind Joe. What was happening? The guard had looked past Joe with a blank stare. As if he was . . . invisible.

Joe started to speak, then closed his mouth. Cautiously he moved toward the turnstile. One step. Two steps. He could see the anxious faces of his companions waiting just beyond the crude barrier. There was the train whistle. His friends frantically waved at him. "Hurry!" one called. "We'll miss the train!"

Would there be shots behind him as the guards suddenly realized what was happening and he raced toward his group? But Joe heard nothing except the ancient engine building up steam. Unhindered, Joe and his fifty Bibles entered Communist China, sprinting along with his companions to make the train to Canton.

During the next two weeks, Joe continued to worry as he and the others toured China, seeing ancient temples and other historic sites in Canton and Beijing, even secretly visiting house church pastors. His companions had unloaded their contraband the first evening in Canton, but Joe had to lug his Bibles around for a full week until a pastor came for them in Beijing. Would the police bang on Joe's door one night and arrest him? But nothing happened. (As it turned out, Joe's Bibles had a special destination, and perhaps that's why they needed special protection. They were destined for Inner Mongolia, a vast land hundreds of miles from civilization that had never before received the Word of God in the Chinese language.)

Two weeks later, Joe and his companions lined up at the same border station, ready to leave China. Everyone quickly passed through—except Joe. This time, instead of being invisible, he was the center of attention. An armed guard took him to an interrogation room. The group leader, Mark, who spoke Chinese, accompanied Joe.

"What is the problem?" Mark asked.

Joe was perspiring. Perhaps his fervent prayer of two weeks before had not been answered after all. Perhaps he *was* going to jail.

The guard held up Joe's passport and visa. "These are not stamped," he explained. "This means you never officially *entered* the country. So how can you exit?"

Of course! Joe had gone into China without being seen. His papers did not reflect the required entry date.

"It must have been an oversight," Mark pointed out.

"We do not make mistakes," an official stated.

What other explanation could there be? Joe and Mark turned innocent gazes upon the frowning Chinese guards, who went to the other side of the room to confer. How Joe wished he could become invisible now! *Lord, don't leave me,* he prayed silently.

And again, the answer came: *My grace is sufficient.*

Finally one of the guards returned, took Joe's passport, and affixed the current date. Then he turned the gears back on the stamp to the date Joe had entered China and stamped the entry box with the proper date. Wearing a sheepish expression, he handed the passport back to Joe. "I guess we are all human," he said. "Have a safe trip home."

When Joe returned to Fuller Seminary and related his story to a group of missionaries, he learned that many other "Bible smugglers" had been supernaturally protected from danger, perhaps most notably Corrie ten Boom, a Dutch citizen whose family hid Jews in their home during the Holocaust until they could be smuggled out of Holland. Corrie was arrested and sent to Ravensbrueck extermination camp because she would not reveal the location of her home's hiding place. She brought a little Bible with her, hanging on a string around her neck, even though the penalty for possessing a Bible was a doubling of one's prison sentence. Not only did Corrie pass through the search lines without being noticed or touched, she kept the Bible in her cell for months and even used it in clandestine worship services for the other inmates. The guards never saw it.

"God is serious about getting His Word to those who need it," Joe Weikel says today. "I didn't fully realize it then, but I do now. His love and mercy never fail."

Like Joe, Richard Tomasello, a lieutenant in the Scranton, Pennsylvania, Fire Department, has never considered himself a hero. He would tell you that climbing into burning buildings, rescuing people, and sometimes running out of oxygen are things that just go with the job. But he does his share of praying just the same. And, like Joe, he knows that God can move air and space whenever He wishes to do so.

One day in January 1997, Richard's engine company was called to a house engulfed in flames. "There's someone in there," one of the men called to Richard.

"I'm going in!" he responded.

Richard searched the bedrooms first, but no one was there. "Then I turned to enter another room, and the full blast of the fire hit me," he recalls. The explosion was so strong that it knocked Richard's helmet off. And there was no hose line of water here!

He had to get out immediately. "I broke the windowpanes out around me—I could barely see them through the smoke—and when the glass fell, someone below ran and got a ladder and also threw a hose up to me," he says. The fire was roaring now, much too strong to be put out with just one thin stream of water, so Richard kept wetting down the area around him, in hopes of keeping the approaching flames from burning him. Then his oxygen-tank alarm went off. Only a few moments of air left.

"I backed up to the window and tried to get through it," Richard recalls. "There was no chance. It was a real small opening, and I was way too big for it." Richard pushed, pulled, squeezed, and wriggled, while continuing to wet the flames now licking at his coat, but there was no possibility of escape. He was going to be burned alive, right here, right now. If he didn't die of smoke inhalation first.

No. He wouldn't go so easily. "God, please

help," he whispered, then stuck his head through the minuscule opening again. This time he perceived something that had not been there before. It was a touch, all around him, that he could feel but not see. A circular barrier between him and the dangerous heat and flames. Now he was being lifted; now going right through the window!

Richard came out of the opening headfirst, grabbed the top of the ladder, and made his way down to the street. His fellow firefighters stared at him in astonishment. They had been getting ready to go up and get him, they explained, but were taking another route. How had he gotten through that tiny window?

When they took the ladder down, they had another surprise. The top few rungs were completely burned. The flames had obviously leaped out the window while Richard was trying to get out of it. Richard's white lieutenant shirt collar, sticking out from under his protective coat, was entirely black too.

Yet, although his helmet had fallen off, and the flames had been all around him, he had no burns—nor any soot—on his head or face. It

was as if he had been enfolded in powerful, protective arms. The situation seemed impossible.
And yet it had happened.

Richard's wife, Joanne, had the answer
when he related the story to her that night. "It
was a miracle," she said simply. And why not?

Mysterious Ways

> *I fled Him down the nights and*
> *   down the days,*
> *I fled Him, down the arches of the*
> *   years . . .*
> *And in the midst of tears, I hid*
> *   from Him.*
>
> —*FRANCIS THOMPSON*
> THE HOUND OF HEAVEN

Of course God loves all His children the same. But He reveals Himself to us—and calls us to His side—in many different ways.

For example, Craig Turner had always been a "searcher," abandoning his Presbyterian roots in favor of Buddhism and Taoism; studying Nietzche and Sartre; and finally embracing atheism in his late twenties. In 1991, Craig was working in Washington, D.C., and one day ran into his friend Beth and her husband, Steve. "Craig, would you be interested in going to Europe with us for about a week, to a small village in Yugoslavia?" Beth asked.

The idea appealed to Craig. He'd been to Europe before and always had a good time. "But why Yugoslavia?" he asked. "Especially with the civil war going on there now?"

"Well . . . people say that Mary, the mother of Jesus, is appearing to villagers in Medjugorje every day, and miracles are happening so that people will believe," Beth explained.

Craig was not at all interested. "I had worked with Beth, and I knew neither Beth nor her husband was strange or fanatical, but I was definitely suspicious of these so-called sightings. I believed that any sort of supernatural or spiritual phenomenon could be explained scientifically and was certainly not indicative of a higher power."

During the next few weeks, Craig tried to talk his friends out of their plans. They had never been to Europe and had paid a large sum for the trip. What if some con artist was taking advantage of them? "Come with us and see for yourself," Beth and Steve pleaded.

"No, thanks." Craig laughed. "The next time I go to Europe, I'll visit Spain. But I'll be looking forward to hearing about all the *miracles* you see."

The day after the couple returned from Yugoslavia, Beth asked Craig to meet her for lunch. "How was Medjugorje?" he asked as soon as he saw her.

"Incredible."

"You mean you weren't disappointed?"

"Not at all. Steve actually stared into the sun for twenty minutes."

"But that's impossible," Craig pointed out. "Anyone who did that would burn their retinas."

"Yes," Beth nodded. Her face seemed to glow. "Except that's one of the miracles that happens there. And we smelled marvelous roses, in unexpected places . . . That's another sign from Mary, that she's near you."

Craig was a bit shaken. He had expected Beth and Steve to return from Medjugorje disillusioned and embarrassed, ready to embrace his belief that there was no God, and that our material universe is governed by the laws of physics. Instead, their faith seemed stronger than ever. "Well," he said quietly, "I'm glad you enjoyed it."

Craig tried to forget about Medjugorje and the questions it raised. But one day, unexpectedly, he felt an intense inner urge, perhaps something like a call to holiness. *Pray, pray, pray,* it said, as if a neon sign was flashing those words, blinking on and off. Craig ignored it. But the prod came back, firm and unyielding, at odd moments. Finally, Craig acquiesced, just to rid himself of the inner prodding. "Hello," he said, lying on his bed one night. "It's me again."

Craig continued to pray, but he was not living a holy life and he knew it. As Labor Day 1992 approached, Craig and his girlfriend, Kathleen, decided to go camping in a remote region of Ontario. The first few days were beautiful, as they hiked and canoed around Ragged Lake. But on the morning of the third day, they awakened in their tent to the sound of distant thunder.

Light rain gave way to heavy rain, then

close-by thunder and flashes. "Are we going to get struck by lightning?" Kathleen asked.

Craig laughed. "No chance. There are too many tall trees here." But a moment later, Craig was hit by "the most incredible pain from every side, surging through my body. I knew it was my moment of death, like the electric chair, and I was screaming as loud as Kathleen. A few seconds later, the pain stopped and everything went black."

Several moments later, the two regained consciousness. They were paralyzed, numb, and terrified. It took at least five minutes for feeling to come back into their bodies; ten minutes for them to feel as if they would, indeed, live. The inside of the tent smelled smoky, from the burns on their clothes and Craig's singed hair. "When we finally reached a hospital, the doctor didn't believe our story," Craig said. "But for the next week we suffered from odd symptoms."

Because of this lingering shakiness, Kathleen, a Catholic, decided to get some comfort by going to confession. "Do you want to come along?" she asked Craig.

"Sure," he said. "I'll drive you."

After Kathleen's confession, the priest spoke with her and Craig for a while, then went over to his closet and emerged with two platinum medals on chains. "These are Miraculous Medals," he explained. "They commemorate events that took place a long time ago." He blessed the medals and slipped them over Craig's and Kathleen's heads. The meeting was over.

Somehow, the medal felt . . . nice to Craig. He got in the habit of slipping it under his T-shirt in the morning. It certainly couldn't do any harm.

About a week later, Craig began to have strange feelings. Not physical symptoms, which he might still attribute to injuries from the lightning. "This was sort of a gnawing or tugging at me inside. Thoughts of Steve and Beth kept popping into my mind. I couldn't get rid of the idea that they were praying for me."

"Kath," he finally said to his girlfriend. "This is strange. I think I have been feeling Steve and Beth praying for me."

"What do you mean?"

Craig described the nameless hunger that seemed to be satisfied only when he prayed, a strange sense of warmth and protection surrounding him at odd moments, hoping Kathleen could explain it all away with some scientific answer.

"I suppose," she said, "that you *could* be feeling them praying for you."

Was such a thing possible? Probable? Would it matter if anyone prayed for an atheist? *Was* he still an atheist? What kind of atheist prayed—and wore a Miraculous Medal?

A few weeks later Craig, Steve, and Beth were out shopping together. It would have to be now, Craig decided. When Beth went to put some parcels in the car, Craig felt a strong inner urge: *Ask him. Ask him.*

"Steve," he said. "Have you . . . have you been praying for me?"

Steve looked at Craig matter-of-factly, as if he had been waiting for the question for a long time. "I sure have."

"I knew it!" Craig shouted as Beth came back. "I felt it. I really did."

"We believe you." Steve laughed. "We said prayers almost daily for you, your conversion . . . sometimes we thought you were a hopeless case."

"Especially when you yelled at us once and told us we were fools for believing in God," Beth added, grinning.

Craig offered a belated apology.

"Craig, do you know what prayer we were saying for you each day?" Beth asked. "The Miraculous Medal novena."

"The Miraculous . . ." Craig yanked the Miraculous Medal and chain out from under his shirt. "Do you realize I was given this by a priest just a few weeks ago—before I had ever heard of it?"

"God works in mysterious ways," Steve said. Who could disagree?

But God wasn't finished sending signs to Craig yet. About a month later Craig popped into Steve's apartment to pick something up. There was a strong aroma of roses permeating the entire place. "Wow, where are the flowers?" Craig asked. "I smell roses." The scent was so strong that he felt as if he was standing in a florist's shop.

"I don't smell any roses." Steve shrugged. "And Beth doesn't wear rose perfume."

"Steve, the aroma is all over the place. Don't tell me you can't smell it!"

"Nope." The two men looked at each other. "Craig!" Steve said. "You're being visited by the Blessed Virgin Mary!"

Craig remembered the story about Medjugorje. But it was incomprehensible, unbelievable. He didn't *want* these bizarre things going on in his life. Yet the fragrance of roses remained (though only Craig could detect it) for half an hour and reemerged again in his car on the way home. The very next day Craig made an appointment with the priest who had given him the medal. Hopefully this man could shed some light on what had been happening to Craig.

Yes, there had been a lot of dramatic experiences in a short period of time, the priest agreed. "These little gifts from God, called graces, are used to convert people who may be close to conversion but need that extra push," the priest explained. They don't happen constantly—because then there would be no need for faith and people would obey God in order to receive a "prize," rather than because they loved Him.

Craig *did* love God, he suddenly realized. And how gently God had set out His path for Craig and led him down it. It had started with the information and intercessory prayer of two friends willing to risk ridicule by "standing in the gap" for him. It continued with a near-death experience that had not hurt them but *had* started Craig and Kathleen thinking about how they should be living their lives. A meeting with a priest who had introduced Craig to Christ's mother. A special sign that she loved Craig as she does all her children, despite his denial of her . . . Craig knew he was just beginning his education. When he left the priest, he went out and bought a Bible.

Today, Craig is a Catholic, married to Kathleen, and a member of a vibrant prayer group in the Washington, D.C., area. His journey consists of small steps of faith, steps that he will take daily until he dies. For him, for all of us, this is the path of conversion.

Just in Time

[God] will not let any of your
anguish go to waste. Instead he
will raise you up and use you
for his purposes, making something beautiful out of every tear
you shed.

—*ANN SPANGLER*

AN ANGEL A DAY

Charity Smith★ grew up in a Christian home
and went to church every Sunday and
Wednesday. "When I was in the ninth grade,
my mother decided that God was calling her to
attend the North American Baptist Seminary in
Sioux Falls, South Dakota," Charity says. The
family moved from Iowa to South Dakota.

About that time, Charity's health began to

fail. Excruciating headaches limited her ability to function as a normal teenager, and she dropped out of most outside activities. Depression plagued her too, but doctors weren't able to get to the root of it. Charity had always hoped to be a model after she finished school, but how could she pursue such a demanding career without energy and enthusiasm?

"We believe that Satan was involved—I feel he is active in the world today and will do anything in his power to bring Christians down," Charity says. "The whole idea of spiritual warfare is too far-fetched for many churches or Christians to believe or understand, but I thought maybe Satan was attacking our family because of my mother's new ministry."

As the end of Charity's senior year in high school neared, her headaches and depression increased. "I seemed to have lost the ability to deal with even the simplest of problems," she recalls. "But like most teenagers, I didn't say much about this to my parents. I don't think they knew how down I was." One morning at school, a migraine began to take over. "I lost count of how many pills I took that morning to try to make the pain go away," Charity says. "But finally I walked into my dad's office—he was the school's band director—and begged him to take me home." Charity's dad was something of a stoic where illness was concerned. But he gave in and drove her home.

"I remember standing in the kitchen listening for the sound of his car pulling out of the driveway," Charity says, "and I have a hard time remembering what went on after that." But she knows that she screamed at God. Hadn't she always loved Him and been an obedient daughter? Why had He deserted her? What had she done to deserve constant pain, both mental and physical? If He wanted her to die, why didn't He just get it over with?

Die . . . Charity's mind felt clouded as she walked to the bathroom and reached for a razor. She could make that happen herself, to finally put an end to the pain. The first few cuts on her arm felt almost good, "like a release." Soon all her suffering would be over. God didn't care about her. Why should she respect His authority?

Then, suddenly, she surfaced from her haze

to see both the bathroom bowl and her arm covered in blood, and . . . what was happening? She heard a pounding at the front door. Had her father come back? She would have to answer it.

She put her arm behind her, went downstairs, and opened the door. There were two women standing there, both smiling at her. Neither of them introduced themselves. "This world is a hurting place, isn't it, dear?" the first one said.

Charity gulped and nodded.

"But, you know, God loves you very much," the other chimed in.

"Where is He now?" Charity demanded.

"He's right next to you," the first woman answered. "He will never leave you, even though it might sometimes feel that way. He'll be with you every step of the way. All you have to do during the bad times is just wait and pray."

"You are not to give up so easily," the second admonished.

The first woman handed Charity a brochure. "Thank you," Charity answered automatically. The two women turned around to leave, and Charity shut the door.

She felt amazingly peaceful now, composed and whole, though baffled. She could see through the front door curtains, but there was no sign of the two women outside. Why had they come to her house; how could they have sensed what she was going through? Had they seen her arm? If so, why hadn't they commented about the blood all over her shirt?

Charity's headache had begun to fade during the encounter with the women, so she went upstairs to treat the cuts on her arm. She counted more than thirty-five of them. Had she not taken care of them or kept on slashing herself, she surely would be dying by now. Instead, she cleaned up the bathroom, put on a long-sleeved shirt, and went back to school.

"When I came home later that day, I quickly ran upstairs to read the pamphlet the women had given me, but it was gone," Charity says. "I looked everywhere for it, with no success. Nor could I remember what the women looked like. But how could I have forgotten, when they had saved my life?" Had the experience been a dream? No, her arm still bore the razor's marks, and she obviously had lost control in the bathroom. "I think God had been listening after all, and He sent two of His angels to save me," she says.

Charity battled depression for another year or so, but she has now conquered the illness and, at twenty-two, models all over the world. "It still amazes me to see how strong and healthy I have become," Charity says. "I hope my experience will help others who face depression to rise above these depths and to remember that there is a Light and we are never left to fight alone."

Perhaps one of the most tragic happenings to hit any family is the suicide of one of its members. And, according to the statistics, the suicide rate continues to climb. Grieving friends and relatives are left with the feeling that they should have been able to predict it or do something to stop it or that heaven should have intervened. "Where were the angels when my friend killed herself?" more than one person has asked.

There are no easy answers. We know that we have free will and, under most circumstances,

God and the angels will not interfere with our choices. Charity was stopped before she could carry out her suicide. But many are not. Why? God is the only one Who knows and, ultimately, the only one to judge the situation.

Those who experience a suicide in their families or friendships, who do not feel certain that their loved one is in heaven or that they will ever see him or her again can certainly pray for that person. And maybe the following story will help.

"My experience happened in a dream," says Dennis Higgins, "so it may be easily discounted by those I share it with. But it was unlike any dream I have ever had before or since."

After suffering from depression for many years, Dennis's sister Trish committed suicide at the age of twenty-nine. Her family grieved but also worried: Had Trish been condemned for all eternity because she had taken her own life?

Shortly after Trish's death, Dennis had a very unusual dream. He and his wife were in their backyard, playing with their child. "I went alone to the side of the house, where I saw a little boy I didn't recognize," Dennis recalls. "Right behind him, walking down the street in a pink evening gown and looking very happy, was Trish. 'Where did you come from?' I asked her."

"A wonderful place," Trish told him.

"What is it like there?"

"Would you like to see it?" Trish asked. "This little boy will take us."

In the dream, Dennis agreed. It seemed as if they were flying. Soon they approached green hills and trees, quite beautiful, surrounding a city of lights. Then they descended and entered a room. There were many people there, all dressed formally and getting ready for some kind of celebration. "Where's God?" Dennis asked.

"Oh no, not here, not yet," Trish explained.

In my Father's house there are many dwelling places. . . . Dennis suddenly comprehended that he was visiting an interim area; the people here had cut their life plan short through their own choice and would thus have to wait a while before they could see God and begin eternal joy.

Dennis hugged his sister and found the little boy, who led him back to his house.

Such an explanation is probably not theologically correct. But perhaps Duane Miller, who regained the use of his vocal cords, sums it up best in his book, *Out of the Silence*:

"I've tasted the allure of suicide. It's not an abstraction to me. I've smelled its breath, I've been drawn by its easy release, and through that experience I can say to any of you—those facing physical ailments, . . . financial cataclysm, and vocational rupture—God never stops being God. He has a future for you. Admittedly, for some of you that future may be in heaven, but that's not for you to know, at least not now.

"Don't short-circuit His process."

From Sir, with Love

*While mortals sleep, the angels
keep their watch of wondering love.*

—PHILLIPS BROOKS

B ill and Marcia Holton and their three children lived on a wheat ranch in Oregon;
Marcia's parents, Verne and Kay, lived next
door. The two homes were at the bottom of
Juniper Canyon, with some of the wheat fields
up on top of the hill behind the houses. "Our
neighbors out here are spread apart, and the
nearest small town is Helix, ten miles from our

ranch," Marcia explains. Sometimes it seemed as if their family were the only people on earth. Occasionally Marcia got a little lonely, but she was a woman of faith who prayed regularly that God would watch over her family. So far He had not disappointed her.

It was a beautiful but muddy Sunday afternoon in early spring, and Marcia had flung open the kitchen door, put boots on the kids so they could run anywhere they wanted, and gone outside with them. The promise of warmth and sun was all around them; planting had begun . . . Marcia loved this time of year.

"Mommy, look!" Her six-year-old was pointing to the top of the hill behind the house.

Marcia squinted. There was an animal up there, sitting calmly and looking down at them. It was huge, at least two hundred pounds. A bear? Marcia thought not—its fur was yellow and fluffy. A mountain lion? "Walk real slowly toward the house," she whispered to the children. "Wait there, and don't come back until I tell you."

Then Marcia took a careful step toward the animal. She knew she would have to investigate before she'd feel safe letting the children play outside again.

Why . . . Marcia could hardly believe her eyes. It was a dog! The biggest dog Marcia had ever seen, probably part mastiff, part Saint Bernard. Where had he come from? Marcia knew all the folks in the Helix area, and no one owned a dog like this. Was he friendly? "Here, boy . . ." Marcia put out a tentative hand.

As if he had been given permission, the dog got up and trotted down the hill directly to Marcia. He allowed himself to be petted, his ears to be scratched and—once she had called the children over to him—to be ridden on and hugged. "Isn't he nice?" Marcia said. "What shall we call him?"

"I think we should call him Sir," one of the children suggested. "Because he deserves respect."

The dog *did* seem regal. Now all that was needed was permission to keep him. The family could hardly wait for Bill to get home from plowing.

"Oh, come on—he won't eat much," Marcia teased that night. "Look at him—isn't he cute?"

" 'Cute' isn't quite the word I'd use," Bill responded.

"But he seems to love us a lot, Daddy," their five-year-old pointed out. "As if he's always been ours."

"Well . . ." Bill was definitely weakening. Although his in-laws had two blue-heeler dogs to help with the cattle they raised, Bill's family didn't own one. And what better place than a ranch for such a big dog? "But we'll have to run a notice in the lost and found in case he belongs to anyone," Bill said. "And if we have to give him back, I don't want any arguments." Everyone agreed.

The cabbie probably didn't know today would be his final Sunday on earth when he went to work this morning, Paul White★ mused, as he lounged in the backseat, his pistol pointed at the hijacked driver's head. But White wasn't going to leave any witnesses to his last robbery. The clerk in the Walla Walla convenience store hadn't seen his face—he'd locked her in the storage closet before he emptied the cash register. But there hadn't been much cash, and he was going to have to pull another job soon.

More important, however, was finding a spot where he could hide for a while. He was an escaped convict on the run, and out here in Oregon, the little homesteads were so few and far between that he could easily dispose of the residents, then portray himself as a visiting relative or friend if any nosy neighbor happened by. Eventually he'd commandeer another car and driver, just like this one, and set out again, working his way east. The police would never find him, not if he stayed out of sight long enough.

The cab driver's hands were shaking. "I-I know you told me not to talk," he said, "but we've gone sixty miles and my gas gauge is on E. I was already low when you pulled the gun on me, and . . ."

White looked out the window. They were passing a wheat field, which looked down into a canyon. At the bottom were two houses. He could see no other dwellings for miles in any direction. Perfect. He could wait up here until dark, and then . . . "Turn into this field," he told the driver, who obeyed just as the engine began to sputter.

White watched the families move about the two houses from his new perch on top of the hill. He considered strategies. He couldn't afford to make a mistake in judgment, because he had very few bullets left. Ultimately, he had to get far away from here, before the authorities in Washington figured out where he had gone.

It would have to be tonight, when they were asleep and unprepared. White looked back at the terrified cabbie and reached for his gun. If anyone in those houses did hear the shot, White reflected, they would probably assume it was just a hunter bringing down a rabbit.

That night, while the Holton family was debating on whether Sir should sleep in the house or the barn, the massive canine settled down easily on the porch across the back door threshold, as if he'd done so always. There was no point in trying to move him, and quiet eventually descended on the household. Until a little after midnight. Then Sir started to bark. What started as just a few short yaps was soon followed by growling, then howling.

"Sir, stop it!" Bill called through the window screen.

Sir obeyed, but a few minutes later the whole process started again.

"What is the *matter* with that dog?" Bill asked irritably. He got up again and looked out the porch door windows. There was no sign of a wild animal. It wasn't all that unusual for a coyote or badger to run through the yard and set off a brief chorus of barking from the dogs next door. But tonight Bill's in-laws' dogs were absolutely quiet.

"Maybe he's homesick," Marcia suggested.

"Wouldn't he be whining?" Bill asked. "This sounds more like aggressiveness. Sir, be quiet!"

Again, Sir obeyed, but only for a moment. He refused to leave the back door to go in search of what was bothering him. But he also barked and growled continuously, as if keeping something at bay. It was almost dawn before the adults in the two households fell asleep. "None of them were very happy with Sir or me that morning," Marcia recalls. "But we all agreed to let him stay one more night."

That day Marcia and the children played with Sir continuously. No matter where they went on the ranch—into the barn, across the road—he accompanied them. "When we were in the house, Sir would lie in front of the door. Nothing could get him to move—until we came out of the house again."

That night, Sir barked only a few times. Marcia relaxed. He seemed to be settling into his new home and she was delighted about it. She loved him already in a way she had never thought she could.

A few days later, Marcia's dad, Verne, was on his way to town when he passed one of the wheat fields and saw something shining. It looked like a car windshield. There shouldn't be any cars there . . . Verne drove closer until he spotted a taxi with Washington license plates on it. Something was definitely wrong, and Verne wasn't about to investigate by himself. He turned around, drove home, and called the state police.

"Get your family and your rifle and lock your-
selves in one of the houses. Don't open the door
for anyone," Verne was told. The police were
on their way.

Slowly, over the next several hours as the
authorities investigated, Bill, Marcia, and her
folks tried to absorb the shocking story. On
Sunday, an escaped convict from Washington
who had that morning robbed a convenience
store had forced a cab driver to take him just past
Helix, to the Holtons' wheat farm, where the cab
driver was then murdered. The sheriff took
Marcia and Bill up the hill, about a hundred feet
from their back porch, and pointed to footprints,
several cigarette butts, and a discarded cigarette
package. Marcia was shocked. The killer had
obviously stood here in the dark, perhaps on
several nights, waiting for a chance to come down
and . . . Marcia didn't want to think about it.

But why hadn't he done so? "I think the only
thing that saved you all was that dog sticking to
you like glue," the sheriff pointed out. "If White
was running low on bullets and had to get past
Sir's attack before he could get to you . . ."

"He'd also lose the element of surprise," Bill

commented. Bill had complained about Sir's noisiness. But what would have happened to them if Sir had not warned the criminal to stay away? What would have happened if they had not adopted Sir?

No one knew where Paul White had gone. Later it was discovered that he had flagged down another farmer, taken him hostage, and repeated the scenario as he made his way across the country. He killed one more person before being caught in Pittsburgh about a week after he had left the Holton farm. Immediately he was sent back to prison in Washington.

No one ever discovered Sir's former owners. The dog stayed with the Holtons for about a year before everyone sensed that it was time for him to move on. Ultimately he went to live at the fire station in town.

Why was the Holton family spared and not the unfortunate hostages? Another mystery, for we know they were loved exactly the same. But as Marcia notes, "In the Bible, it tells us that if we pray, God provides angels for our protection." Perhaps Sir was not really an angel. But that he was sent from heaven, Marcia has no doubts.

Our God Reigns

> *God is to me that creative Force,*
> *behind and in the universe, who*
> *manifests Himself as energy, as life,*
> *as order, as beauty, as thought, as*
> *conscience, as love.*
>
> —HENRY SLOAN COFFIN
>
> NEWTON: MY IDEA OF GOD

Barbara Shleman Ryan was working as a nurse at St. Francis Hospital in Evanston, Illinois, several years ago, when she began to feel compelled to pray over people. She had an insight that they needed not only to be physically cured but to be healed and the two are not always the same. So, as she administered medications and bandages, she also prayed. The results were compelling. The patients she cared for seemed to go home sooner.

Gradually Barbara developed a healing ministry. God seemed to work through her whenever she laid her hands on people. And Barbara began to realize that people were not the only ones who needed healing—in many cases, the earth itself was in need of it. For example, Barbara points out, there are parts of the world today where violence has occurred, yet—although wars may have been over for a long time—very little vegetation still grows. People should be blessing those areas. "Indians have recognized this need for a long time, receiving prophecies that the Great Spirit wants to cleanse the earth again, this time through fire," she says. "But that sounds so ominous; couldn't the cleansing be the fire of the Holy Spirit instead?"

A few years ago, after she and her family had moved to Florida, Barbara's prayer group kept receiving a prophecy that God wanted a healing center built in the area. It should be on the water and accessible to everyone. No one in the prayer group had the slightest clue as to how this could be managed or accomplished. But rather than dismiss it, Barbara thought the idea warranted more intense prayer. "We needed to make a corridor of light to the heavenly kingdom," she says. "So I enlisted two friends and we began to pray about the idea every Tuesday morning for a few hours. We would, in effect, say, 'Lord, if this idea is from You, please bring it to fruition. If not, please let us know.'

"We met regularly every Tuesday for eighteen months." The women occasionally inspected a building or some property, but everything they saw was either too expensive or too far away.

On one particular morning, however, one of the women received what she suspected might be a message from God. He was asking their little group to request forgiveness for what had been done to their Indian brothers and sisters. The women were puzzled, since they knew no Indians and hadn't had any contact with them, but they obeyed. Within minutes, each of them was gripped with a terrible sadness. They wept, overwhelmed with sorrow and repentance.

"It was obvious that some of our ancestors or people of our heritage had brutalized some Indians somewhere," says Barbara. "It didn't really have to make sense—we could just feel that God wanted us to make amends for their suffering."

A day or two later, as one of the women was running errands, she passed a piece of property right on the water. *Now that's just what we need for our healing center,* she thought, then slammed on her brakes. A Realtor had just approached the front of the land carrying a big FOR SALE sign. The price was right, and the prayer group ended up buying the land and started to build their long-awaited healing center.

One day Barbara decided to call on the neighbors who lived near the land and explain what the group was doing. "Since this land was located in the original part of the town, I figured I'd also learn some things about its history," she says. And she did.

"Interesting thing about that parcel," the elderly lady in the house next door told Barbara. "It used to be a burial ground for the Indians who died during the seven-year Seminole War. Their tribe was almost decimated—by American soldiers who took their land."

Shocked, Barbara remembered when the

prayer group had been inexplicably led to atone for some sort of transgressions against Indians. "Perhaps no one had ever repented for destroying this tribe, especially if it had been done in God's name," she says. So when the group prayed that morning, they cleansed the land of the sorrow and pain it had borne, just as a group might pray for the healing of a *person*. Thus restored, the land was then ready for God to renew and bless and use again for something positive.

Many times we haven't realized that the healing responsibility is extended to all of creation, not just people. But everyone lives where there has been some pain and violence, or perhaps has stayed in a hotel room or an area of a city where grave sins have taken place. A simple blessing or prayer over such a space can cleanse it. And an area or item needn't be sinful in order for us to bless it. A recent story in an Iowa newspaper detailed a group of farmers who gathered to pray over their livestock and seed in hopes of a bountiful year. A growing number of people bless their own homes too, not only asking God to protect the house (and send angels to live there) but declaring it a sacred space, where anger, pain, and suffering will be curbed as much as possible.

This is also why many people feel confident (after asking God's permission) to pray to subdue the weather. "We can speak to things in the environment that aren't going our way," Barbara says, "because we are God's sons and daughters, and He has given us dominion over the earth."

She remembers in particular when she and several others were invited to a Crow Indian reservation outside of Billings, Montana, to give a conference on healing. About a thousand Crow had gathered in the open rodeo grounds with just a light tent covering it, and mass—said by the bishop—had begun. Suddenly a tribal policeman hurried over to where the conference team, including Barbara, was standing.

"We've just heard that a tornado is headed this way," he told her. "It's already hurt a lot of people. You've got to stop and let everyone get to safety."

Safety? Barbara looked frantically at the flat plains surrounding the meeting place. Where was safety? *Only in God's arms . . .* came the answer. Well, Barbara had never asked for a miracle this huge before, but she and the other speakers began to pray quietly in the back of the tent. "God, You are Lord over all the earth. We will take control over this tornado in Your Name and stay in the tent. Please protect us all and calm the winds as Jesus did."

When the bishop had finished his homily, he was also informed of the danger. He too led the assembly in a prayer to hush the storm, adding, "Let there be nothing but a soft rain all night long."

Time passed. Barbara and the others heard a lot of thunder and felt a bit of wind, but gradually everything died down. By the time mass had ended, there was nothing more than soft gentle rain, which lasted all night and seemed to symbolize the cleansing action of the Lord.

The next morning, everyone was able to see the destruction—fallen trees on either side of the rodeo grounds. As the *Billings Gazette* reported it, the tornado had raged on a straight path through the land until it reached the rodeo grounds. There it had inexplicably split in half, zoomed around the tent—knocking down trees as it traveled—then joined again and continued its rampage.

It's important, however, to pray over nature as God would intend it. For example, Barbara recalls the time when a hurricane was heading straight for Miami. Her first thought was to pray that God would divert its direction. However, she soon remembered that Miami had been in a drought condition for many years. "We needed rain but not destruction," Barbara says. So the prayer group convened all Saturday night—as the hurricane came closer and closer—to pray protection over their land. About five miles off the coast, the hurricane suddenly stopped. Within hours it had blown itself out, then moved gradually up the east coast of Florida, dumping much-needed rain along the cities there. Only minimal destruction of property resulted.

We don't often use this authority, do we? But, as Barbara says, we can. "We need to be sensitive to the promptings of the Holy Spirit, sometimes in dreams or through Bible readings when we are being asked to pray, especially for someone or against destruction. But don't ever forget, we're asking God to make this earth just like it is in heaven. We're getting it ready for the Lord to come back."[5]

Mellissa Miles of Portage, Indiana, certainly wouldn't have believed that such a thing was possible. In fact, she didn't know much about God at all. But when her little girl was about two, Mellissa and her husband began to think more about what kind of religious beliefs they would be passing down to their family. "Although we were married in the Nazarene church, I hadn't gone regularly since I was about fourteen," Mellissa says. "We started attending Sunday services the winter our daughter turned two and then I decided to take a Monday night course called Naza-What? It was a three-part series that explained our church's beliefs."

On the second Monday, shortly after a heavy snowfall had ended, the class broke up about 10:00 P.M. and Mellissa left soon afterward. Because she lives about five or six miles from the church, she would sometimes opt to take a gravel back road—even though it has a deep ditch on either side—in order to avoid some red lights. This night, however, she hesitated. Much safer to drive through the well-lit, well-plowed section of town. But . . . much faster to take the gravel road. She turned onto the back road despite the ditches.

"I had gotten about halfway home when I became engulfed in a very thick fog," Mellissa remembers. "It wrapped the car in a film and I couldn't see where the gravel road ended and the snow-covered ditch began. In fact, I couldn't see more than a few inches in front of the car." Her headlights produced strange, disorienting shapes, which confused her even more.

No streetlights. House lights too far away to be seen through the fog. No way to turn around or look through the rear or side windows . . . And what if she went down a ditch and the car rolled over, pinning her inside?

Mellissa grabbed the steering wheel in a death grip and drove about two miles an hour, lurching each time she hit a hidden dip. She had to get off this road. But she couldn't see a thing!

"Suddenly I remembered our pastor's talking

tonight. About how God wanted us to bring all our problems and fears to Him. Even the littlest things, even if we don't think He would do anything about them. So I immediately began to pray. 'Lord, I am so scared. Help me to see. Make the fog go away, please. . . .' "

Instantly the fog cleared in front of Mellissa's car. Her mouth dropped in astonishment. Had it simply lifted? But no. The fog was just as thick along the side and back windows as it had been before she prayed. No visibility at all. But a narrow clear view through her front windshield was leading her to safety.

"The little path remained open for me until I turned off that road toward my house," Mellissa says. "And when I looked back, I could not see down the road. The fog was dense again."

Although Mellissa had not specifically taken authority over the fog, she had done precisely what her pastor had suggested: asked God to command the weather for her. And He had.

There are those who believe that the next few years will bring some difficult weather catastrophes—tornados, floods, earthquakes, and other types of disasters of an intensity and frequency that our country has not previously experienced. Perhaps it has already started, if one considers the recent meteorological results attributed to El Niño. The reason usually suggested for this theory is that God is trying to get our attention by lifting His protective hand from our nation, which was founded on religious principles that today are seemingly ignored or even attacked. Whether such problems will continue, only God knows. But it may be helpful to remember that we can pray over nature, ask for shields and protection from the elements, and place ourselves confidently in His hands.

The Other Passenger

*Heroism is the brilliant triumph of
the soul over the flesh . . . the
dazzling and glorious concentration
of courage.*

—HENRI FREDERIC AMIEL,
JOURNAL, 1 OCTOBER 1849

The late Corrie ten Boom, at the age of
twelve, had told her father that she did not
think she could ever be a martyr. "I would be
afraid of the pain," she admitted. "So I would
deny my belief in God—or say anything else
they wanted to hear."

"Corrie," her wise father responded, "when

you and I go for a trip on the train, when do I buy the tickets?"

Puzzled, Corrie answered, "Why, just before we leave, Papa."

"Exactly. There would be no point in me buying them three months ahead of time, since we wouldn't need them then. Am I right?"

"Yes, Papa. But what . . . ?"

"And that is the answer to your dilemma, too. For if you were ever asked to be a martyr, God would give you the grace to go through with it at the time. You don't have the grace now, because you don't need it now."

So it is with many heroes. They don't start out as heroes, but somehow the voice of God intervenes. And they find themselves during a crisis taking risks for Him that they never would have dreamed of taking otherwise.

For example, Ed and Anne Gove and their nine-year-old son were on their way back to their home in Westford, Massachusetts, from a satisfying vacation in Florida. They had enjoyed the time off but were now beginning to turn their thoughts back to reality. "Ed is a mechanic, and although I've had some nurse's training, I now manage a salon," Anne said. "I was thinking about the people who had taken charge for me—had everything gone all right for them? Ed was probably wondering the same thing."

Then, without warning, their son pointed ahead. "Look!" he shouted. On the shoulder of the road sat a car in flames. What was even more incredible was that no one had stopped to investigate or help. What if someone was *in* the car? "Dear God," Anne prayed quietly, "we need Your help." Ed pulled over behind the distressed vehicle, as Anne had known he would. Ed was not the kind of man to pass someone in trouble. The two of them tumbled out and ran toward the vehicle. Wildly, Anne waved at cars passing by. A few pulled over, but no one got out to help. The flames were almost completely covering the car by now.

"Anne!" Ed called. "There's someone in the front seat. But the flames are so thick, I'm afraid the gas tank is going to explode any minute."

Anne abandoned her attempt to enlist a helpful motorist and ran to assist Ed. Putting her face as close as she could to the driver's side, she shouted: "Is anyone in there with you?"

There was a pause. Had the driver died already? Then, almost in a sob, came the answer: "Jesus. Jesus is here."

"Oh, Ed." Anne's eyes filled with tears. "We have to try to save her. I—I just can't stand here and watch her burn to death."

Ed nodded grimly. The victim sounded young. If he and Anne were able to pull her out and she died anyway, at least her family would know that someone had been there for her. He started to pray as he reached inside, dodging the flames. The woman was apparently lying on the front seat floor, stuck between metal parts and shattered glass. And the fire was so hot! How was Ed going to manage this?

Anne kept praying—Ed could hear her as he wrenched and pried pieces away from the girl, jumping back every few minutes to avoid the flames. "God, let us get her out before the car explodes," Anne continued imploring. During the times when Ed would move aside, Anne reached in to help pull. At one point, Ed singed his own clothes. Would they be forced to give up?

But no. All of a sudden something gave way, releasing the driver. Ed lifted her as gently as he could, up and out onto the grass, as far away from the car as possible. A moment later the car exploded, blowing the trunk lid off. The woman was unconscious and badly injured. But if medical help came soon, Anne believed she might recover. The woman's eyes flickered and Anne leaned close to her.

"Was anyone else with you?" she asked again.

"Jesus was there," the woman murmured before lapsing again into unconsciousness.

Jesus would have had *to be there,* Anne thought, sitting back on her heels as she realized the full impact of what had happened. The car was thoroughly in flames by now. Ed's hands were cut, and he was suffering acutely from smoke inhalation, but he was safe. Somehow they had managed to free a victim from a hot tangle of metal and steel without losing their own lives, when no one else was willing to help.

Eventually the paramedics arrived. Although they wanted Ed to go to the hospital for treatment along with the victim, he refused. "After that long drive and now this, I just want to go home," he told Anne. And they did.

The young woman lived, despite a difficult recovery. Anne and Ed had the satisfaction of meeting her family, receiving everyone's thanks, and knowing that, without their help, the story would have had a much different ending.

"We didn't really think about the why of it too much," Anne says today. "We got involved almost automatically, because we would like to believe that if we ever needed help, some stranger would get involved and help us."

But that sudden surge of grace and energy, they know, could have only come from the other Passenger in the car.

Home for Christmas

All is calm, all is bright . . .
—"*SILENT NIGHT*"

Patricia Cleary,★ a geologist, was teaching environmental health and safety classes for a small business in Maryland when the Persian Gulf War erupted. Because of her husband Tom's★ active-duty status and their preschool daughter, Patricia changed jobs and took one that did not require traveling. Cy Miller filled her old position.

"In the beginning, it seemed that things wouldn't work out for Cy," Patricia recalls. "I stayed a part-timer with the original company; I was popular with the students. Cy was someone new. He took a lot of heat in the beginning from this close-knit, practical-joking bunch."

But gradually Cy made inroads. A proud army veteran, he was gentle and funny, too, and the four or five pens always stuck in the placket of his company-issue shirt became an endearing trademark. Patricia grew to love him.

Patricia's little girl, Catherine, was not immune to Cy's charm either. "One of the exercises we use to train students to decontaminate after a chemical incident is to put them in the 'man from mars' suit and pour chocolate syrup on them—which is dark, sticky, and hard to scrub off," Patricia explains. One day when Catherine was at the office with her mother, Cy allowed her to douse several of the students with syrup. Catherine was ecstatic. "She loved and trusted Cy instinctively, and they became great friends," says her mom.

In late 1993, however, Patricia noticed that Cy's energy seemed to be lower than normal.

Soon the word was out: Cy had cancer. He underwent chemotherapy and seemed to snap back, healthier than before. A year later, however, Cy reentered the hospital.

Although by that time Patricia hadn't seen Cy in months, she kept in touch via frequent phone calls. "You're going to beat this," she reassured him regularly. "We're all praying for you."

"Keep it up!" Cy would say.

On December 22, while driving home from a business trip, Patricia's thoughts turned again to Cy. What kind of a Christmas would he have, stuck in the hospital? She ought to visit him . . . Impulsively, she pulled onto the Baltimore beltway and drove straight to the hospital. But when she got to Cy's room, she barely recognized him. "Cy was thin, wasted away, not at all the vigorous man I remembered," she relates. "I knew he was expecting to die, and he wasn't afraid." But Patricia was devastated. All the reports about him from her colleagues had been very hopeful—no one had revealed what was obviously happening. "I realized now that none

🖾 232 🖾

of us could bear to part with him." And yet when they said their good-byes, it was almost as if he knew this life would not go on much longer. "He seemed happy and at peace," Patricia says. "I was the one who was sad."

It was going to be a terrible Christmas, Patricia thought as she drove home. And what was she going to tell Catherine? Her daughter knew that "Mr. Cy" was sick. But Patricia hadn't explained much more than that to her six-year-old.

Christmas Eve was a busy, bitterly cold day, as Patricia tackled her holiday tasks. More things needed to be wrapped, and some holiday cooking remained. She and Tom would have to assemble Catherine's Dreamboat Barbie after their daughter went to bed. Patricia knew she should try to feel happier. But how could she? *God should have a rule against people dying at Christmas,* she thought.

Catherine must have been thinking of Cy too. "I'm going to draw some pictures for him," she announced brightly after lunch. "He can hang them around his hospital room. Will you bring them the next time you visit him?"

"Of course," Patricia assured her. But she wondered if there would *be* a next time.

However, at 2:00 P.M. Catherine abruptly stopped crayoning. She looked up from her project, frowned slightly at something unseen in the distance, and put the paper aside. "I won't finish this one, Mommy," she said. "Mr. Cy doesn't need it anymore."

"Okay." Patricia, knee-deep in cleaning chores, barely acknowledged Catherine's comment.

A few moments later, a friend from the office phoned. "Cy just died," he told Patricia. "At two o'clock."

Two o'clock. Patricia looked at her six-year-old. *Mr. Cy doesn't need it anymore,* Catherine had said. How could she have known?

Patricia remained calm until Christmas Eve services. "No one had notified the church that Cy had died," she recalls, "so, by mistake, the lector read prayers for his healing." Patricia started to sob quietly in the pew, hoping no one would notice. Cy hadn't been healed. Why? Hadn't they all prayed well—or hard—enough?

Tomorrow should be such a joyful day—but how could it be?

Little Catherine fell asleep easily, and Patricia and Tom assembled the rest of her toys and laid them beneath the tree. The house was still frigid due to the zero-temperature outside. "Is there any way we can turn the heat up?" Patricia asked Tom as they got ready for bed.

"Afraid not," Tom answered. "That old furnace just can't keep up with this cold."

Patricia couldn't get warm, even under a thick layer of blankets. Maybe her trembling was actually delayed shock and sorrow, she thought. How was she going to get through tomorrow, especially when grief was going to keep her up all night?

But no. She *had* fallen asleep, because now she was waking up again. The room seemed bright—was it morning already? Patricia rubbed the sleep out of her eyes, sat up, and looked toward the brightness. Cy was sitting at the foot of her bed.

"He looked plump and healthy, just like he always had before he got sick," she says. "He was wearing his usual company-issue shirt, with four or five pens stuck in the placket, as always, and there was a warm glow all around him. I remember feeling embarrassed because I was wearing a nightgown and I didn't think he should see me like that."

"I'm just fine, Patricia," he said. "I know you're upset, but I don't want you to be."

"But Cy, we're all going to miss you so much . . ." In spite of this incredible, unbelievable scene, Patricia felt tears springing to her eyes.

"I understand your sorrow. But please don't let it ruin Catherine's Christmas. Or yours." He was smiling, in the jovial, heartwarming way he always did. "Be happy, Patricia, because there's no need to grieve."

This couldn't be happening. But it was. Patricia reached over to Tom and shook him. "Tom, wake up!" she whispered. "Look!"

Even as Tom roused himself, however, the light faded. Cy was gone. But something of him remained. "Have you noticed," Tom asked, "how warm it is in here, all of a sudden?"

Christmas morning was the most joyous of times, for Patricia had been given a gift of great worth. She had been healed of her grief. And now she realized that the prayers she and others had offered for Cy hadn't been wasted after all. Cy had been healed in the best possible way. He was home for Christmas, borne on the wings of angels and the love of his friends.

Tina's Angels

> *. . . These truants from home and*
>   *from heaven*
> *They have made me more manly*
>   *and mild,*
> *And I know now how Jesus could*
>   *liken*
> *The kingdom of God to a child.*
> — *CHARLES MONROE DICKINSON*
>   *"THE CHILDREN"*

Tina Soldan was young when she married in 1985, but old enough to believe that what she was feeling was true love, despite her husband's unstable temper. Raised in a faith-filled Baptist church, Tina felt certain that God loved her and that He would help David★ conquer his anger problems and become a loving and responsible husband.

"Our marriage was rocky almost from the beginning," Tina recalls. "I miscarried my first pregnancy, but three months later, I became pregnant again. Then the trouble began in earnest."

David had decided that he did not want to be a father. He became increasingly violent, both verbally and physically. He accused Tina of being pregnant by someone else and frequently threatened to kill her. Tina repeatedly called the police, but during that time period, police were often reluctant to get involved in domestic disputes and thus took no action. After baby Lesley was born, David's outbursts increased. Occasionally, he even threatened the infant. Still hoping that God would restore their union, Tina hung on for a while. But when Lesley was two, Tina discovered that David was being unfaithful to her, and it was the last straw. The couple separated.

Tina could not afford a divorce just yet, but she enrolled in college, received her nursing degree, and went to work at a local hospital. Her mother came to her apartment each day and cared for Lesley. When Tina did file for divorce, David, prompted by his own mother, decided to fight for custody or extended visitation rights. "The court proceedings were ugly, lasting about a year," Tina says. "We had to go through mental health evaluations, and although every expert said David was not fit even for visitation rights, he received them anyway."

It was a difficult time, and Tina often wondered where God was. Hadn't she done her best to carry out His will? Tina knew a loving God would not want her to endanger herself or her child in a violent marriage, and she was at peace with her decision to leave. But her spiritual faith had been shaken. How could something so bad happen to a woman who had tried to be so good?

Then, to her relief, David seemed to fade from the scene. Tina heard that he had been convicted of stealing firearms and had been sent to jail in a nearby community. He served a brief sentence, was released, went to Georgia, and promptly committed another crime. This time he was sent to prison there. Tina began to relax.

Perhaps her former husband would be locked away for several years and—except for his mother, who believed Tina was responsible for her son's problems and often harassed her with late-night phone calls—life might settle down.

Early in September 1991, after Tina returned home from work one evening, her mother approached her. "Tina," she began, "has Lesley mentioned her 'friends' to you?"

"Friends?" Tina asked. "You mean the kids in her kindergarten class?"

"No. I mean *angel* friends. She's been talking about them a lot this past month."

"Oh, Mom." Tina smiled. "You know how little children are, always making up stories. I wouldn't take that seriously."

Mrs. Soldan frowned. "I think you should. I think something's going on."

Perplexed, Tina went to Lesley's room, where her daughter was playing contentedly. What did Tina's mother mean? "Tell me about your new friends, Lesley," Tina asked.

Her daughter looked up, eyes shining. "You mean my angel friends?" she asked. "Mommy, there are lots of them, all around! And they

play with me, and sleep near me, and go everywhere with me."

Angels? "Lesley, you shouldn't say things
that aren't true," Tina admonished her.

"But it *is* true." Bewildered, Lesley looked
around the room. "Can't you see them? They're
children just like me, but they're so pretty!"

A chill ran up Tina's back. She went to see
her mother. "I don't know what to think," she
admitted. "Lesley's never told lies before. But
how would she even know about angels? They
haven't taught the little kids anything like that in
Sunday school yet . . ."

"Angels are real," Mrs. Soldan pointed out.
"They're in many books of the Bible. Why
should we assume that she *isn't* seeing them?"

True. But Tina and Lesley were just ordinary people. Why should guardian angels be
hovering around *their* house? She wouldn't say
anything more about this to her daughter, Tina
decided. She would simply watch and wait.

Weeks passed, and the angel activity seemed
to increase. According to Lesley, they were
everywhere, at the dinner table, in the car . . .

Rather than joking, her daughter's attitude was solemn and sincere, Tina noticed. Lesley even confided that the angels wished she would behave a little bit better at school! Would she make all this up? Tina wondered.

Then one day Tina received a call from a local assistant district attorney whom she had met during her divorce proceedings. "Did you hear about David?" he asked.

"David?" Tina was instantly alarmed. "What about him?"

"He was released from jail, and he told the prison authorities that he was coming up here to kill you."

"Oh, my God!" The nightmare was starting all over again.

"Calm down, Tina. It's all right now. When he didn't show up for his probation hearing, they put out a bulletin on him and caught him. He's back in jail. But it was a close call—he was only a few hours away from here."

She had been in danger, and she didn't even know it! "When did this happen?" Tina asked.

"Last month."

Last month. When the house had apparently been filled with guardian angels. Tina went to find Lesley.

"Lesley?" she asked casually. "What are your angel friends doing now?"

Lesley looked up from her coloring book. "Nothing much," she said. "Most of them are gone."

Of course. There wouldn't be any need for an army of spiritual warriors here, now that David was no longer a threat. . . .

No. Things like this didn't happen. The timing must have been a coincidence. Tina decided to put the whole episode out of her mind.

Several months passed. Then one evening, Lesley suddenly looked up from the dinner table. "Mommy!" she announced. "My angel friends are back!"

"They are?" Tina had almost forgotten.

"Lots and lots." Lesley looked around the room in delight. What did it mean?

Soon Tina had her answer. David had been released from jail again and had been free for about two weeks in Georgia, corresponding perfectly with the visit of Lesley's "friends." The heavenly messengers hadn't stayed very long; they had drifted away at the exact time David was rearrested and sent back to jail on a new charge.

Tina didn't know what to think. Since no one knew about David's movements in advance, how could Lesley invent stories that coincided so precisely with the actual events? Surely it was just a fantasy. And yet, there was something so reassuring about it all. Tina had wondered where God was, during this whole struggle. Was it possible that He had been right beside her all along?

From that point on, Tina began to watch in earnest. And she was not disappointed. "Whenever David was due to be released from jail (although I would usually not know this until later), the angels would be around in force," she says. David's mother had received his visitation rights after he went to prison, and she initiated many court orders—primarily, Tina believes, to harass her. "Each time the papers were to arrive in the mail, the angel friends would be there before I received it. Sometimes the house would seem filled with them; sometimes there were only a few. Perhaps the number matched the degree of danger. They became my signal that something that could affect us was about to happen, or was happening somewhere." This gave Tina time to prepare herself and Lesley for whatever was coming.

One might wonder why the angels did not simply *remove* these troubles rather than helping Tina and Lesley cope with them. Tina originally wondered too. "As in any turmoil, my faith both flourished and faltered," she says. "I had a few friends who were there for me through it all. And I prayed a lot." Gradually she grew calmer. "Although I never *saw* Lesley's angel friends, I did learn to feel their presence and draw courage from it. And I think both Lesley and I are stronger for this whole experience."

Lesley is now almost twelve and says that her angel friends have not been around for quite a while. Perhaps it is because she has grown and no longer sees with the innocent eyes of early childhood. But it may also be linked to the fact that her father has been incarcerated continuously for several years, and that his mother has not served Tina with court papers recently.

"Who knows?" Tina says. "Maybe the angels will be here again someday, hopefully for happier reasons.

"But I will always be grateful to God for their presence and their protection." They came, she says, when she needed hope most.

And a Little Child
Shall Lead Them

> . . . Trailing clouds of glory do we
>   come
> From God, who is our home:
> Heaven lies about us in our
>   infancy!
>
> —*WILLIAM WORDSWORTH*
> *"ODE ON INTIMATIONS*
>   *OF IMMORTALITY"*

As we've seen, children do seem to have a special spiritual awareness, at least during their early years. Carol Biddle of Windsor, Ontario, has a daughter who manifested many typical behaviors. "When Meaghan was a baby, I learned not to go to her right away when she awakened because she liked to spend time alone in her crib—and even seemed somewhat annoyed when I 'interrupted' her," Carol recalls. Meaghan would talk for long periods of time in "baby babble," but with pauses, as if she was listening to someone respond. "As she grew, she had several invisible friends, all with different names and personalities. They would go with her everywhere, even needing to be 'buckled up' when we got into the car. Meaghan also had an odd way of guessing who was on the phone or at the door before I answered it. When she was two, she told me I had a baby in my tummy—and I did, although I didn't yet know it."

When Meaghan was about four and a half, she announced, "When I turn five, Ghostie"— her main imaginary friend—"and all my other friends will disappear. Invisible people don't live past five years old."

They did indeed disappear after Meaghan's fifth birthday, Carol says. "And we have not heard of them since. Meaghan also quit telling me who was at the door or on the phone. It was a sad time for my husband and me when Ghostie, Katrina, and the other friends left us."

Children also seem to interact frequently

with those who have died. Since they are too young to fear this transition, perhaps it seems quite normal to them. Jessica Morello, now a teenager, was about seven when her beloved grandmother died. "I was grieving as I fell asleep one night," she remembers. She didn't know how she could bear this loss. Had Gram truly gone away forever? "Then, in the middle of the night, I awakened, and there was Gram sitting at the foot of my bed, her arms open to comfort me."

The two played some games and had a party featuring their favorite menu—cherry Kool-Aid and Gram's special white whipped-cream cake. "Gram told me that she would help me through the rough times to come and, no matter what, she would always be with me," Jessica says. The little girl fell blissfully back to sleep.

The next morning, it would have been a simple matter to dismiss Jessica's experience as a dream. Except that Jessica awakened to her father's concerned face as he bent over the bed. "Jessica, how did all these red stains get on your pillowcase?" he demanded. "And you've got white icing on your cheeks!"

———

Mary Ann, a friend of mine, lost her sister to cancer. The young woman left an eighteen-month-old son. One day when Mary Ann and her nephew were shopping in the produce section of a large market, the little boy suddenly straightened up, pointed, and with face aglow turned to his aunt. "Look, Aunt Mary Ann!" he cried joyfully. "There's Mommy!"

Mary Ann turned to look in the direction her nephew was pointing. There was absolutely no one there, not even a shopper. And yet this child remained elated throughout the rest of the day. "I saw Mommy!" he told anyone who would listen.

Some experts believe that children do indeed have visions—of angels or loved ones in heaven—during their early years, and that such episodes wane as the child moves into more worldly activities. Yet "perhaps we [all] carry this memory unaware throughout our life," observed the great Christian mystic Agnes Sanford. "Why else the deep nostalgia, the wave of homesickness for heaven that sweeps over us at unexpected moments?"

There are even evidences of prenatal awareness. Interviewed on ABC's *Prime Time Live* in October 1997, the mother of the famous Dilley sextuplets commented that all through her pregnancy, everyone was anticipating five babies. They were astonished when a sixth—Adrian—emerged; he, never seen during ultrasound, had been hidden behind Mrs. Dilley's spleen. Yet as her brood learned to speak, each of them told her that they had seen Adrian "when we were in your tummy."

And in another instance, one of my readers, seven months pregnant, was involved in a frightening automobile accident. She was taken to the hospital, treated, and released, with apparently no damage suffered by her unborn baby, either. Although the mother never mentioned this accident to her daughter, the infant would begin to cry whenever they passed the site of the collision. And as she grew, the child would tell her mother, "This place scares me. I didn't like that crash."

Because children do seem to be "heaven-connected" in special ways, it makes sense to develop their natural spirituality early, believes Helen Beason, who has been an educator for more than twenty-five years as well as a children's pastor. Several years ago, Helen came across a passage from Deuteronomy that had a profound effect on her. "Take these words of mine into your heart and soul," the lines read. "Teach them to your children, speaking of them at home and abroad, whether you are busy or at rest." Helen thought about the typical children's church programs, not only in communities of which she had been a part but across the country. Rarely, if ever, were children being recognized, raised up, and trained to be prayer warriors; few of them were exhibiting changed lives as a result of religious instruction. Because educators generally assumed that youngsters would have neither the ability nor the interest in intercessory prayer and worship, they limited teaching to Bible stories or, as Helen puts it, "the same old thing in new packages. But there just had to be more."

Helen believed that a fertile spiritual field was being ignored. "It has been common practice to place only adults in areas of prayer, service, and ministry," she says. "Yet the Scriptures give us plenty of examples of children and teens being used by God in mighty ways. Youngsters raised within a strong spiritual family today are waiting—no, *straining*—to become effective members of the body of Christ, not to sit on the sidelines until they are older." After all, as she points out, the Holy Spirit—if allowed to do what He wants to do—can teach *all* ages and compete with any of the worldly enticements our children face.

In early 1992, Helen was children's pastor at the Living Word Church in New Wilmington, Pennsylvania, and decided to try out some of her theories. She started by encouraging expectant parents within the church community to read the Bible, sing hymns, and pray *aloud*, so their unborn children could hear (just as the tiny John the Baptist leaped in his mother's womb when he heard Mary approach and speak). "The parents were excited to try something new for their unborn infants," Helen says. "Later, several couples saw a distinct difference between the 'prayed over' child and their older children."

When tots came to the nursery on Sunday mornings, "we put away the baby-sitting mentality," Helen says. Instead, workers prayed blessings over each child, recited Scripture, and played worship music. Toddlers were trained to lay hands on one another and pray for one another. Things did not always go smoothly, but the adults began to notice a calmer, more receptive attitude among the youngsters. One twenty-month-old actually implored his mother at home, again and again, to "pray—Rachel!" Although his mother wasn't sure just what was going on, she prayed with her child each time he asked. Later, the adults discovered that Helen's teenage daughter, Rachel, serving in a mission in France, had been hospitalized. No one could have known she was in distress, except the Holy Spirit—who passed on the need for intercessory prayer to a child still in diapers!

Noting the success with the church's toddlers, Helen wondered about the older children, especially those ages four through twelve. She felt certain God was asking her to form and train them, too. But how? And would any be interested? On July 19, 1992, she put an announcement into the church bulletin about a new group forming: SWAT (Spiritual Warfare Advance Training). "If your child desires to become a mighty warrior for God, bring him to the trailer room thirty minutes before the main service next week," the ad said.

Helen assumed that a few children would be dragged to the meeting, just because their parents wanted to show their support for her. She was not, however, prepared for twenty-five young recruits, most so enthusiastic that they had persuaded their parents to bring them early. But as the group began to pray, spontaneously, without explanation or specific format, Helen could feel the strong presence of the Holy Spirit. Several children suddenly received the gift of tongues, a new prayer language. Others told Helen of their deep-seated longing to participate more fully in the Kingdom.

Helen was overwhelmed. During the next several months, as membership climbed to sixty-five children, she and the other leaders taught their small charges how to pray over one another or for those far away (some children would actually hold a globe and weep, interceding for unknown youngsters in foreign lands), to stay focused and listen for God's directions, to pray in tongues, and to read Scripture with thoughtfulness and faith. The children became comfortable breaking into small groups of four or five to pray over someone as a team. Gradually they moved into preservice prayer, participating with the adults before the main church service.

A year later, Helen added a weekday meeting night to the SWAT schedule and expanded the age range to four through eighteen. "Even now we do not separate by age but work with the whole group," Helen says. "It is not uncommon for even the youngest to participate with a prayer, a vision, or a prophetic word." As the children get older, they are appointed junior staff members or are sent out with the adult staff to visit other kids "and help them catch the flame of excitement in serving the Lord in active ministry."

While Helen was busy training children in Pennsylvania, Sue Young of Bradenton, Florida, was receiving a similar message. A youth pastor working mainly with teenagers, she began to get one of those inner urges that so often means a prod from God. "I sensed that He wanted me to work with younger children in some capacity," she says. "But I liked teens and was trained for that age group. I was afraid if I prayed about it, I might actually get the answer I *didn't* want. So I ignored the whole thing."

Sue had recently moved to Bradenton's Christian Retreat Center, a nondenominational international training center for conferences, with a church, mission programs, and even housing for people who wish to live within a Christian community. Sue was an administrative secretary there at the time but still worked with teens whenever possible.

"One night I was asked to substitute for the teacher who taught fifth- and sixth-grade girls," Sue recalls. "I didn't want to get involved with that age group but reluctantly agreed to help out." At the beginning of the class, everyone started to pray. And then Sue watched in amazement as the Holy Spirit seemed to sweep through the room—just as the Bible describes Pentecost. Some of the girls began to weep. "God wants us to lay hands on the sick," one said. "We all know He does. He wants us to use the gifts He's given us *now*, and not wait 'til we're all grown-up." Several of the girls fell to the ground, while others began to pray in tongues. Sue sat open-mouthed. She had been at similar meetings with adults, and certainly knew of the power of the Holy Spirit. But she had never experienced anything like this involving children.

The meeting ended prayerfully, but Sue wasn't quite sure what to think. She was convinced of the girls' sincerity, but she wasn't their teacher and had no authority to establish this type of format. "And I didn't want to admit that God *was* probably calling me to minister to younger children," she says.

But the following night, Sue was asked to sub again—this time, for the fifth- and sixth-grade boys' class. And again, the same mighty manifestations occurred. The boys were as powerful and prayerful as the girls had been. What was going on?

By the following week, when the third- and fourth-grade teacher resigned and Sue was "coincidentally" asked to take her place, Sue saw the writing on the wall. God was doing something in this community, and she would have to follow His lead.

Sometime later, the founder of the Christian Retreat Center returned from a trip to Pennsylvania, and he called his staff together. In astonishment, Sue listened as he told the group about a woman he had met—Pastor Helen Beason—and the amazing things happening with the children in her church. "Wow!" Sue exclaimed. "I have to meet this woman!"

Sue called Helen immediately. Not only was Helen planning a vacation—to Florida!—but she was leaving that very day. Sue had phoned her just in time, and ultimately the two women met. Eventually, Sue and her staff brought some of the children to Helen's training camp. "God really inspired them," Helen recalls, "and when they went back to Florida, they took the fire with them." With Helen's help, Sue formed another branch of SWAT and now has several hundred active members. "On Saturday mornings, we go to the housing projects and the migrant workers' camps, and our children—sometimes more than a hundred of them—

conduct a Bible school, complete with praise and worship and praying over the project children for healing and help," Sue says. "It's amazing to see it. There seems no limit to what God is allowing the kids to do today."

Meanwhile, across the country in River Forest, Illinois, in April 1996, Tim Holmes, a young husband and father, was facing devastating news. He had been diagnosed with non-Hodgkin's lymphoma and was receiving chemotherapy treatments. "A great deal of love was being poured out on us at this time," Tim recalls. "My wife, Jan, was a spiritual and emotional rock, as were my in-laws, Jackie and Jerry Spierenburg, who had left their own work at the Christian Retreat Center in Bradenton, Florida, to move into our home and take care of whatever needed doing." Friends rallied around, and people from St. Luke's parish as well as the First Presbyterian Church, where Tim's children attended Sunday school, offered support and prayers. Tim's business partner took over the running of the office. But when the chemotherapy treatments ended in September, physicians found a new tumor in Tim's chest. There was nothing to be done now except a bone marrow transplant, followed by radiation and an experimental therapy, interleukin-2.

"The whole process would take four months and be mentally and physically challenging," Tim says. "But we decided to go ahead with it and, once again, people came to our aid, even offering their own bone marrow, blood, or platelets, if needed." Tim attended another healing service and was prayed over in several different churches. He was ready for the surgery.

But Tim could hardly have imagined what was about to happen. His insurance company denied the claim, protesting that interleukin-2 would probably not eliminate Tim's cancer. His physicians argued otherwise, saying his odds of being cured were at least 30 to 40 percent. Because the company had given Tim no other medical options, the insurers then agreed to a further review. But this could take weeks, even months, and Tim did not have the luxury of time now.

"This was the darkest hour," Tim recalls. "And yet, everywhere I looked, people were still praying and helping. A lawyer offered to fight the insurance company for me, pro bono. My business partner wanted to help me pay for the transplant. I felt God's presence in a close, tangible way—my faith had awakened, and an enormous amount of spiritual healing had taken place in my life. We decided to place ourselves in Jesus' hands and await His will on this whole matter."

By October, Tim's in-laws, the Spierenbergs, had returned to their home and work in Bradenton, Florida. For the moment, at least, there seemed nothing more that they could do in River Forest, and there were many things that needed doing in Bradenton. One day at church, Jackie ran into Sue Young. Sue had three ten-year-old girls from the SWAT team with her. "How is your son-in-law doing?" Sue asked.

Jackie explained the situation. "We're very worried," she said.

Sue looked thoughtful. "The children here should be praying about this," she said, beckoning to the three girls. Quickly she explained Tim's situation.

The children thought for a moment. "Let's pray that the cancer will dry up and go away," said one.

Another nodded. "Then the doctors won't have to do this awful thing, so the insurance company won't have to pay."

The third smiled and put her head back. "I can hear the doctor saying right now, 'Tim, why are you even here?'"

How simple. The children prayed as they had learned to do, commanding the sickness to leave. "Dry up and go away!" each one said. The entire SWAT team continued to pray for Tim's healing for the rest of October.

At the end of October, Tim sat in the doctor's office. They were getting nowhere fast, he realized. The insurance company was remaining firm in its decision. And Tim was concerned. He was certainly running out of time, yet saddling his family with such a huge debt—especially if the surgery wasn't successful—seemed unwise.

The doctor had just rerun tests to see how far the cancer had progressed during this time of waiting. Now he opened the office door, looking baffled. "Tim? I'm not sure how to tell you this . . ."

Had it gotten *that* much worse? So soon? "Yes?" Tim asked urgently.

"Tim, there isn't any cancer. None. There's no point in even scheduling the transplant."

"But . . ." Tim was astonished. "How could a chest tumor just disappear?"

"You must be in remission," the doctor told him. "Go home and enjoy it."

There is a statistical probability of relapse in almost half of those with Tim's type of cancer, so Tim is not taking a moment of his life for granted. But although he continues to be closely monitored, no sign of his cancer has returned. "Regardless of what the future holds, God has enriched and blessed my life and my spirit beyond measure," he says. "I have become a witness to His glory."

At the time of this writing, there are about twenty-five SWAT-inspired children's prayer teams in the United States, as well as groups in Zambia, Zimbabwe, Kenya, and India. "God is moving powerfully worldwide, with children, teens, and adults. He is not leaving anyone out," Helen says. But children have that simple faith quality; they believe and are ready to act on their beliefs, she says, just as they did for Tim Holmes. "I believe they will have a great part in ushering in this harvest, the greatest harvest the world has ever known."[6]

Moments of Love

Coincidence is God's way of remaining anonymous.

—*UNKNOWN*

Grace Douvres grew up on a farm in Cornwall, England, where being with the animals was the best part of her life. But her career ultimately brought her to New York City, far from the green hills and hedgerows she had taken for granted for so long. Life in New York was exciting, especially after she met and married her husband, Jim, but she still missed her "critters."

One evening Jim came home from work with what appeared to be a lump under his overcoat. Grace was curious. "What have you got there?" she asked.

Jim grinned as he withdrew a tiny kitten, frail, dirty, and mewing plaintively. "She followed me upstairs from the subway," he explained sheepishly.

"Oh!" Grace was overjoyed. This was the cutest, sweetest, most adorable kitten she had ever seen—well, she would be, just as soon as Grace gave her a bath and nursed her back to health.

"We named her Bonnie because she was such a little 'bonnie belle' of a cat," Grace recalls. "Every day she grew more precious and delighted us with her antics. I thanked God again and again for sending the perfect little companion for me." And if Grace wasn't already pleased enough, Jim brought another kitten home one evening during a raging snowstorm.

"I think a neighbor abandoned him," Jim

explained. "I couldn't leave him out there to starve, could I?"

"Of course not," Grace assured him. Privately she wondered if their home would soon become an animal shelter, but Jim apparently felt that two cats were enough. The second, which they named Heathcliff, settled in quickly. But despite her affection for Heathcliff, Grace loved Bonnie best.

As Christmas approached that year, Grace began to notice advertisements looking for people to become foster parents to a child in a poverty-stricken area of the world. "Adopting" such a child meant sending a certain amount of money each month to ensure that the child would receive food, clothing, and an education. The child's guardian, in turn, would send a report on the child a few times each year. The idea appealed to Grace. She researched several places and decided on the one she would like to support. But life was busy, and the application remained on her desk.

One morning Grace noticed that Heathcliff seemed lethargic. He refused his food, ignored his toys and, by evening, seemed terribly ill. "It sounds like feline leukemia," the veterinarian told Grace when she phoned. "You'd better bring him in first thing in the morning."

"Oh, no!" Grace knew what that meant. There was no cure for this virus, and cats were usually put to sleep right away to spare them the pain associated with it. She would have to give consent for that, if necessary, to spare Heathcliff any more suffering.

The following morning Jim took Heathcliff to the veterinarian. The cat was not able to come back home. "And be careful," the vet warned Jim. "Not only is this illness fatal, it's also highly contagious."

Bonnie! Had she caught it from Heathcliff? Grace worried all day.

Within the week, Bonnie was exhibiting the same symptoms as Heathcliff had. She was sluggish, had no appetite, and was disinterested in things around her. Grace was devastated. She had little doubt that her cuddly companion had caught the fatal virus from Heathcliff. She would have to have her pet put to sleep. There wasn't any other choice.

Except . . . She could *pray* for a healing for Bonnie. She did. "It was a very tearful and apologetic prayer," Grace recalls, "because for some reason I felt guilty about asking Him to heal a cat."

As she prayed, she noticed the unmailed foster parent application on the desk. "I'll mail this tomorrow," she promised God, "so I can take care of someone like I'm asking You to take care of Bonnie. And . . . if You do heal her, will You send me a sign that it wasn't a coincidence, that it really came from You?"

The following morning, Grace was amazed to see Bonnie pitter-patter over to her food dish and whine to be fed. A few hours later, she was throwing her rubber mouse in the air. "Jim!" Grace called. "I think Bonnie is getting well!"

Although it was never determined that Bonnie had feline leukemia, she did recover completely and never exhibited symptoms again. Was God responsible for this? Grace can only remember the "sign" she requested when she prayed for her cat's recovery. It came a few weeks later, from the foster parent organization.

"Thank you for becoming a foster parent,"

the letter read. "We have assigned you a little boy from the Philippine Islands. His name is Bonnie Sotio."

"This event comes under the heading of the wonders of God, I think," says Grace. "Not terribly dynamic or startling, but just another indication of the love our Father has for us."

Sometimes God has to specifically rearrange His natural order—time, space, nature—in order for something to be accomplished. As always, we are left with minds boggled.

For example, about six months before Betty Trotter's mother, Eileen Post, was diagnosed with Alzheimer's disease, Betty had attempted to arrange for Eileen to come from her home in Omaha to Betty's home in Chicago for a visit. Eileen had already shown some signs of vagueness, and Betty was uneasy about the whole trip. But there was no one in Omaha that Betty could ask to oversee the plans. She would have to make the arrangements herself, pray about everything, and trust that God would go along on the trip.

Betty booked Eileen on a flight due to land at Chicago's O'Hare Airport about 3:00 P.M. on a Wednesday. But that Wednesday morning, snow began to fall. When Betty called O'Hare, she learned that her mother's flight had been canceled.

How was her mother, increasingly forgetful, going to understand this? "It took a great deal of patience, repetitive long-distance phone calls, and assistance from a local travel agent before Mom understood that she was to take the same flight the next day," says Betty. On Thursday morning, taking no chances, Betty phoned her mother again. "Are you ready to go to the airport, Mom?" she asked.

Eileen was confused. "Airport? Isn't that on Friday?"

Betty's heart sank. This was going to be harder than she'd hoped. "No, Mom. Remember, the plane was canceled yesterday. You're supposed to take the same flight today. And you need to be ready to go soon."

"Well, all right," her mother agreed.

However, when Betty phoned back, about thirty minutes before her mother should have left for the airport, Eileen was still vague. Was the trip today? No, she hadn't made transportation plans for getting to the airport. No, she hadn't finished packing. Betty convinced her mother to go to the airport anyway. Perhaps once Eileen was there, she could work something else out.

Betty hung up and started to pray. "God, I've got to have some help with Mother. Obviously, she's going to miss this flight now, but can You get her on the next? Please watch over her and bring her here safely." Then she called her travel agent.

"Don't worry," the agent said soothingly. "I'll call the Omaha airport and tell them to find your mom and get her on the next flight; it lands at O'Hare about four P.M."

Betty hoped everything would work out. She ran a quick errand, got to the airport gate at three-thirty—and stopped, dumbfounded. The four o'clock flight wasn't in yet. But her mother was sitting there calmly, waiting for her.

Betty found Eileen's suitcases stowed in an area away from the regular baggage. Later, she learned that her husband had received a phone call from someone identifying himself as an "airline representative," who said Eileen had been found wandering, disoriented, through the O'Hare terminal and was being brought to the gate where Betty had planned to meet her.

Everything *had* worked out. Everything . . . except the timing. For how did Eileen get on the earlier flight—with luggage packed—when she had been completely unprepared just before it left? And was she even *on* that flight, considering the amount of time she presumably spent wandering O'Hare's labyrinthine corridors before someone spotted her, found her son-in-law's phone number among her possessions, stowed her suitcases in an out-of-the-way place, and brought her to the correct waiting area?

"We never discovered how Mother got here, and she didn't remember any of it," Betty says. But God protected her, just as Betty had asked.

Vincent Tan was born Tan Ban Soon in Singapore to Chinese Buddhist parents. As a young boy, Vincent was very interested in science.

One day as he read a book on nuclear physics in the library, he discovered an offer for a Bible course stuck within the pages of the book. Curious, Vincent ordered the course. Ultimately he became a Christian and because he wanted to attend a Christian college, he came to the United States, where he gave himself the western name Vincent.

Vincent graduated from college and took a job in analytical chemistry in Chattanooga, Tennessee. His faith deepened, possibly because he was no longer afraid to share it with others, and life settled down. In March 1993, Vincent was working late in his lab, occasionally looking out the window to keep an eye on his car, since several had recently been stolen from the area. He noticed a stranger standing on the passenger side of his car. The man was young and clean-cut, but thieves come in all guises, and because Vincent is proficient in the martial arts, he felt safe investigating. Stealthily grabbing a long metal rod from the lab, he opened the door and called, "Yes? Can I help you?"

"Hi, Vincent," the stranger responded.

Vincent was startled. Had he mistaken a

friend for a thief? But no, he had never seen this man before. "Do I know you?" Vincent asked.

"Not really," the man responded. "But you don't have to use Chi Sao or the rod on me. And your mother is fine."

Now Vincent was really confused. No one in America knew of his skill in Chi Sao. Nor could the stranger see the rod Vincent held behind him. And who could have known that his mother in China had just developed a heart problem?

The stranger smiled. "You love the Lord very much, don't you?"

"Yes, I do," Vincent answered. He started to relax.

"He loves you, too," the man replied. "And He is coming very soon."

Vincent was thrilled. Could this be true? He looked away for just a second or two, and when he looked back, the man had disappeared.

Could he have been an angel? Eventually Vincent told his story to Jim Bramlett, an author who researches prophecy material, and Jim used Vincent's experience, among others, in a magazine article.

Three years later, on Saturday, April 6, 1996, Vincent awoke at 4:30 A.M. with a strong belief that he was to pray. He wasn't exactly sure about *what*, but this urge had come upon him before, and he always obeyed it. He prayed for a few moments, then fell back asleep.

At seven o'clock Vincent awakened again and began his usual morning prayer time. About a half hour later, his telephone rang. It was too early to answer the phone on a Saturday, he decided, and continued praying. The answering machine would handle the call.

But the phone kept ringing. Insistently. Had Vincent forgotten to turn on the answering machine? No, he could see the red light from where he knelt. Vincent got up and went to the phone. Ten rings, eleven . . . and although the Caller ID was also turned on, no number was displayed. Vincent gave up and grabbed the phone. "Hello?"

"Hello?" It was a woman's voice.

"Hello!" Vincent repeated.

"Hello!" the woman answered again.

"Yes—did you want to speak to me?" Vincent was getting exasperated.

"No."

"Then why did you call?"

"I didn't call," the woman answered, as annoyed as he. "*You* called me!"

He hadn't, Vincent explained. He had simply answered his phone. The very same thing had happened to the woman. She introduced herself as Doris. "I live in Iowa," she said. "I can't imagine how this whole thing happened, Mr. . . . ?"

"My name is Vincent Tan," he answered politely, planning to say good-bye and end this strange mix-up. But the woman gave a little gasp.

"Are you the Vincent Tan who had an experience with an angel?" she asked.

"Well, yes . . ."

"My mother and I read about it in a magazine. We never forgot what a wonderful story it was. Six months ago, my mother was diagnosed with terminal cancer. Every day since then, she has prayed that she might be able to speak with you before she died. This morning I awakened at three-thirty, and I prayed, reminding the Lord of my mother's request."

Three-thirty. Given the time zones, Doris

had awakened at the same moment as Vincent. They had been praying together.

"I can't believe this is happening," Doris went on. "Would it be too much to ask you to talk to my mother?"

"Put her on the phone," Vincent said.

The elderly lady's voice was weak and hardly audible, but for the next forty-five minutes or so, the two talked. Vincent told her about his angel experience in great detail, and they discovered that several of their favorite Scripture passages were the same. Finally, the elderly woman whispered, "Praise the Lord. Amen."

All became quiet. Thinking the old woman had fallen asleep, Vincent was about to hang up when Doris came back on the phone. "Mother has died," she told Vincent. "Thank you for what you did for her."

Vincent was overwhelmed. A soul had just entered eternity, and he had been permitted to play a part in this joyous journey! He and Doris said their good-byes quickly so she could begin the necessary arrangements. It was not until several hours later that he realized he had never gotten Doris's last name or address, nor had the Caller ID recorded the call. Furthermore, Vincent never received a bill for the call, although Doris had told him she had answered *his* ring.

Vincent saw no point in investigating further, for the experience, he believes, was simply part of God's plan. "The Lord has His reasons for all of this," he says. "And as we near the final hours, I know that He is even closer."

When Mary McDonald* learned that her daughter Sheila's father-in-law had died, she grabbed her car keys and went to the store to buy some food for the bereaved family. Who is ever prepared for neighbors and out-of-town guests coming in when something like this happens? "Sandra, our other daughter, sent over a huge salad and two chocolate pies," Mary recalls. "I bought a pan of frozen lasagna that's supposed to serve twelve not-very-big slices and a smaller pan of macaroni and cheese— something that serves about eight or nine. I remember it specifically because I stood in the checkout line for a few moments wondering if it would be enough. But I assumed other neighbors would be pitching in too."

When Mary and Sandra delivered their food, they were surprised to discover that theirs was all the grieving family had received. "I guess folks don't send food to bereaved families like they used to," Mary says. "There were nine people there—all extremely hungry and short on cash. They had enough to go downtown that evening and get hot dogs, which they did. I felt bad that I hadn't sent something for the next morning, because all they had were coffee cakes."

The next evening, however, the family—which by now numbered thirteen—warmed the two pans. "It was strange, Mom," Sheila told Mary later. "Some of these men are big eaters. But we not only didn't run out of lasagna and macaroni and cheese, there seemed to be a lot left over. Everyone said they were absolutely stuffed."

"Maybe someone else delivered the same dishes," Mary suggested.

"No. I was in the kitchen. Your pans were the only ones there."

Mary hung up, briefly thinking of the Miracle of the loaves and fishes. But God didn't do things like that today, did He?

On the following day, before going to the funeral, the family sat down to eat a small meal: the same pans of lasagna and macaroni and cheese. The salad and pies had been long since consumed, but there was still plenty of the main course left. Everyone ate gratefully from over-flowing plates again.

All this time Mary had been feeling a bit guilty about not bringing over more food. "But God never forgets," she says today. "He fills every need if we give Him a little to work with."

Sometimes an angel's help is so gentle that we're apt to miss it if we aren't tuned in. Cyril Phillips and his wife, Marjorie, live in the hilly outskirts of Kalamunda in Western Australia. Cyril sees his brother Mel and sister-in-law Flo frequently, and Mel is always suggesting that the families take a vacation together. "I am not too keen on driving vacations," Cyril admits, "and as the

Christmas holidays approached one year and Mel began to really push about this, I became even firmer in my opposition."

While sawing wood one morning, Cyril heard a voice in his mind. *You are selfish,* the voice said.

"It was an unexpected blow," Cyril said. "I was surprised and hurt." Cyril wondered if the voice was his angel's. "Why am I selfish?" he asked the voice.

Marjorie and David would like to go on a trip, the voice said. Cyril felt sheepish and somewhat surprised. It had never occurred to him that his wife or son would enjoy traveling. But the next time Mel asked about the families sharing a vacation, Cyril said yes.

All arrangements were made, and the families met at Mel's house just as he was securing an oversize load to his large trailer with ropes. It was a beautiful day, but Cyril was a bit nervous at the size of Mel's trailer load: apparently Mel's daughter, her husband, and their baby had decided to go too—with, of course, lots of extra supplies. Cyril believed in angels—hadn't one spoken to him about this event? He would just have to put the trip's safety into their hands.

The two vehicles pulled out, and for a while everything went smoothly as they skirted around the suburbs and eventually reached the highway. "This is so relaxing," Marjorie told Cyril. "I'm glad we decided to go." She settled back again but a few moments later peered forward. "Cyril," she asked, "do you smell burning rubber?"

Cyril looked ahead at Mel's car. "I was horrified to see a back wheel of the trailer actually flapping wildly about," Cyril recalls. Cyril caught up to Mel and motioned him over to the side of the road. Mel followed Cyril's lead and stepped out of the trailer to meet him.

Mel's smile faded when he saw the wheel. He spun around, ran back to the trailer, and soon had jacked it up and pulled the wheel off. The men turned pale. Because the trailer's load had been so heavy, the thread grooves at the end of the axle had been stripped. The bolt could no longer hold on to the thread, even if they replaced the tire with their spare. There was no way they could drive any farther.

Cyril looked around. They were in a little-traveled area, deep into the bush. No houses to be seen, and no one could remember when they had last passed one. They had a baby with them, and a child. It was getting later in the day. Cyril was standing behind Mel. All of a sudden he heard a voice in his head, the same voice he had heard once before. *Mel wants a piece of tinfoil,* the voice said.

Cyril looked around. No one but he had heard the voice. But even if it was something he should pay attention to, what were the chances of finding tinfoil out here? And what good would a thing like that do anyway? What they needed was a new axle.

But Cyril had been a friend of God's long enough to know that he could ask for just about anything. "God," he said silently, "if there's tinfoil out here, and You have a plan for it and us, please show me where it is."

Almost immediately, as if being directed, Cyril walked diagonally across the road, stopped among the dry leaves and picked up a piece of tinfoil that lay there, all by itself, in plain view.

"Here's your tinfoil, Mel," he said, handing it to his brother.

Mel's mouth dropped. "Where did you get *that*?" he asked. "I was just thinking that if I could wrap two pieces of tinfoil around the stripped screw, it would probably hold long enough to get us to a repair station. But who could find tinfoil here in the wilderness? What a wonderful coincidence!"

Not if you're listening to those small voices, Cyril thought as he watched his brother fix the wheel. Once again he thanked the angel who had told him he was selfish. "The incident had a profound impact on all of us, and my faith was greatly strengthened by it," he says today.

Seventh-grader Michael Halas had always enjoyed good health, so when he began running fever after fever, his parents were concerned. Then during one bout, Michael had joint pain as well. His father, John, remembered having read some articles about a newly discovered illness called Lyme disease, which had recently become more prevalent in their Voorhees, New Jersey, community. The symptoms of Lyme disease mimicked many others, including juvenile rheumatoid arthritis, and some patients became very ill or even permanently disabled if the disease was not caught in its early stages. "Could this be Lyme disease?" John Halas asked the pediatrician the next time Michael ran a fever and was taken to the doctor's office.

"Not a chance," she answered without hesitation. "It's just a typical adolescent virus."

The Halas family had great confidence in this doctor, so they hesitated to argue. "But I remember reading something about joint pain being a symptom of Lyme," John persisted.

"It accompanies viruses, too," the doctor assured him. The family went home. On the one hand, they were grateful that the doctor seemed so positive and that Michael would be spared such a serious sickness. But John had trouble sleeping that night. What if they were all wrong?

A few days later, for reasons now forgotten, Mr. and Mrs. Halas exchanged cars. John traveled over one of the Delaware River bridges into Philadelphia from South Jersey. Returning to Jersey later than afternoon, he suddenly saw a piece of paper fly across the hood of the car and wedge itself somewhere under the edge. "It kept flapping like it was waving to me," John says. He sped up, trying to dislodge it, but with no success. The bothersome item hung on for the next fifteen miles, until John was able to get back to his office, park, and get out to see what it was.

The paper was actually a pamphlet of about ten pages, open in the middle, with one half under the rim of the car's hood, wedged so perfectly that it looked as if it had been placed there by hand. Moreover, it was too thick to have stuck under the hood of his own car, had he been driving it that day. John took the pamphlet out, turned it over, and looked at the title. It was a booklet on Lyme disease.

"I ran to my office and read the book from cover to cover," John says. "I then phoned my wife, told her what had happened, and we set off for the doctor's office. I didn't tell the doctor about the booklet then; we just said we wanted a Lyme disease test done ASAP." The doctor agreed, and the family had the results in about three days. The test was positive.

"Michael went on medication for the next thirty days, and the Lyme disease cleared up," John says. "We had caught it in time. Today Michael is healthy, strong, and healed."

Was it just a coincidence that the medical knowledge this family needed was provided to them in such a unique way? You decide.

Heaven in Hazard

> *Whate'er we leave to God, God*
> *does*
> *And blesses us.*
>> —HENRY DAVID THOREAU
>> "INSPIRATION"

Ken Gaub grew up in Yakima, Washington, the oldest of six and the son of a man who at one time had no use for God. But over the years, Ken's parents developed a deep spiritual faith. "I began to see amazing miracles and answers to prayer in my parents' lives," Ken says, "and I knew it had to be because of their commitment to God." And that was fine.

But not for Ken. Oh, he had nothing against religion or the ministry. At times he'd even practiced preaching—"I'd get wound up and do a lot of hellfire and brimstone"—but Ken also had a gift for making people laugh. He was the life of the party and hoped someday to be a professional comedian. He didn't see how both vocations could exist side by side. By the time Ken reached his teens, he was also somewhat of a daredevil who enjoyed taking risks. But God seemed to protect him anyway.

For example, Ken had fixed up an old car and took it out for a test-drive one afternoon. Faster and faster he went, down a deserted road. The gas pedal was almost to the floor when Ken spotted a large cardboard box lying ahead of him in the middle of the road. He would hit it, he decided, and watch it explode all over the place!

"But just before I reached it, I felt the steering wheel turning," Ken recalls. "The car was being taken out of my control, and somehow it went completely around the box without touching it at all." Shocked, Ken looked in the rearview mirror and broke out in a cold sweat. Two little children were getting out of the box.

Ken knew that God had intervened in this situation. He was grateful but still not convinced that he was being called to the religious life. One night, however, Ken's father took the family to see a traveling minister conduct a religious revival in a tent. More than ten thousand people attended, and Ken was spellbound as miracle after miracle took place. On the way home, he announced to his parents, "Someday I'm going to do like that preacher. I'm going to have a tent and preach, and I'm going to help people just like he did."

It was certainly a worthy goal, but many years passed—and a lot of hardship and backsliding—before Ken began to see the beginnings of his dreams come true. He met his wife, Barbara, at Bible college in Washington, married her shortly before graduation, and decided they should leave for Kentucky. "Kentucky?" Barbara asked him. "Why there?"

Ken knew nothing about Kentucky except what he had seen illustrated in books. But his father had once lived there and had often described its beautiful mountains and creeks. "I think a lot of people need us there," Ken told her, so they loaded their old car with everything they owned and set out on their three-thousand-mile journey.

The couple evangelized their way across the country, "but either the people in those cities went to bed real early or had other things to do," Ken says, because their turnouts were small. What if they got to Kentucky and discovered that this was *not* the place God intended them to go?

But once the Gaubs arrived, they discovered that although the people were poor, they were also hungry for education. After Ken and Barbara found a place to live and a place to conduct worship, the neighbors came from everywhere around Hazard to attend, sometimes walking for miles, barefoot despite the danger of snakes. Ken spent hours visiting up and down their creek dwellings and started a Bible school for the children. Money was always short, and Ken and Barbara lived on the edge most of the time, but God helped too. One day Ken had only one dollar to use for gasoline for his car. The attendant put in the dollar's worth, but when Ken pulled away, his tank was completely full. On other occasions, just as they spent the last of their money on food, someone would bring them something to eat. "We simply tried to obey the Lord and bless other people," Ken explains. "The more we blessed them, the more they blessed us."

But of course there were also people, as in any mission field, whose hearts were closed to the word of God. Ken usually respected their beliefs. And yet if someone in an unbelieving family was sick, it was hard for Ken *not* to visit, since praying for healing was, to him, one of the most important parts of his work. One day he met Millie Johnson★ downtown. Millie's husband, Jake, a giant of a man, had told Ken in no uncertain terms several times just what he would do to him if he talked "that religion stuff" with Millie. But now Millie approached Ken with tears in her eyes. "Jeremy's very sick, Preacher," she said. "He's in the hospital." Jeremy was the Johnsons' year-old baby. "Do you think you could go and pray for him?"

"Millie, I'd be happy to go," Ken told her. "But you know how Jake feels about it."

"He's on a trip today," Millie said. "He'd never know."

"Okay." Ken had been heading to the hospital anyway, so he took some extra time to stop in Jeremy's room, lay hands on the baby, and pray for his recovery.

For the next week, each time he made his hospital rounds, Ken kept a lookout for Jake. If the man was visiting with his son, Ken bypassed the baby's room. If he saw Jake leaving, he knew he could stop to pray.

One particular day, the hallway outside Jeremy's room seemed exceptionally quiet. Ken peeked in. No one was in the room, so he tiptoed over to the crib where the baby lay with a sheet on top of him. Reaching out his hand, he softly touched the sheet covering Jeremy so as not to awaken him. "Lord," he prayed, "raise up this baby for Your glory."

Uh-oh. The baby had started squirming. Ken had better get out of there before Jeremy cried and attracted attention. Just as Ken turned to leave, he saw that the doorway was blocked by Jake's very large frame. Jake was glaring at Ken.

"Now, Jake . . ." Ken began.

Then Jake looked over at the crib, and saw

the sheet moving. "Oh, God! Oh, God!" he cried.

Ken tried to think of something to say to placate him and get around him. By now Jake's yelling had attracted a nurse. "Please, sir, this is a hospital," she said to Jake. "Calm down. I realize this is hard on you, but . . ."

Jake continued to yell and point at the crib. Then the nurse looked at the crib, and she screamed. All the color faded from her face as she backed out the door and ran down the corridor. Jake ran over and picked up the child.

Ken was at a loss as to why everyone was so upset. Maybe the baby was dying. Obviously, Ken had made the situation worse, so he left quickly, before anything else could happen.

When the hospital phoned later to say that the parents wanted Ken to return, he assumed that little Jeremy had died—either that, or Ken was going to be reprimanded for intruding. Not knowing what to expect, he was flabbergasted when Jake rushed up and threw his arms around him. "Preacher, I want you to know I changed my mind about that religious stuff. I believe now!" He began weeping again and couldn't say any more.

"What's going on?" Ken asked.

Millie looked at him, tears streaming down her cheeks. "Preacher, didn't you know that our Jeremy had died two hours before you prayed for him?"

"What?" Ken was stunned.

"They had pronounced him dead—they were just waiting for Jake to have a last look at him."

"Well, I didn't know that," Ken explained. "I just felt I had to pray for that baby. I just asked God to raise him up for His glory."

"And God did?" Jake asked.

"We serve a wonderful God, Jake," Ken explained. His heart was full. God had certainly shown him that right here in Hazard, Kentucky, was where He wanted Ken and Barbara to be. And there would be no shortage of signs and wonders, as long as they placed their trust in Him.[7]

The Last Word

*These are the ones who have
survived the great period of
trial . . . and God will wipe
every tear from their eyes.*

—*REVELATION 7:14,17*

Evelyn Heinz, a fellow writer and friend, recently told me an interesting story. She had become a grandmother again, this time to Victor Thomas, born December 27, 1997, in Colorado. Evelyn had been unable to be in Colorado for the birth but was hoping to travel there in March. In the meantime, she wrote a simple prayer asking that God would send angels to guard all her grandchildren, especially this latest addition.

"About a week after Victor's birth, my daughter Amy phoned to tell me that she and her husband, Craig, had taken the baby to their family physician for his first checkup," Evelyn told me. Baby Victor was sleeping contentedly on Craig's lap as his parents sat in the waiting room across from two elderly ladies who were the only others there. Suddenly Victor smiled in his sleep. Could it be a *real* smile, on a newborn? Amy and Craig stared. Yes, there it was again. And again.

Then one of the elderly ladies spoke, enthralled. "Look! There are angels all around your baby!"

It was just the message Evelyn needed. "Since I couldn't be in Colorado yet, I think God let me know He was watching over my grandchildren," she said.

The reactions of everyone involved in this little episode were fascinating, for various reasons. If such a thing had happened as recently as five or ten years ago, I suspect there might have been scoffing rather than acceptance. The elderly lady in the waiting room may not have had the courage to speak up. If she did, she most likely would have been regarded by the young couple as "slightly off." Evelyn might not have thought to ask for angelic protection—or would not have so matter-of-factly accepted her daughter's account as a tender and personal response from God.

But as we have seen in the preceding stories, angel sightings, visions, miracles, and answers to prayer are no longer considered rarities, limited to saints. God is apparently sending forth signs to *everyone,* all over the world. He wants us all to be part of His family.

That, of course, entails a decision. And God doesn't assure us of an easy journey, even if we do say yes. There will be rocky roads, valleys, confusion, occasional suffering. But God *does* pledge that He will always love and bless us, and that He will be with us throughout it all.

What a promise! The King of Kings; the Great I Am; the Alpha and Omega; the God of Abraham, Isaac, and Jacob; Who threw the planets into the skies; Who split the Red Sea and carved the mountains out of the earth . . .

. . . loves *you*.

Hold out your arms. Close your eyes. Open your heart and invite Him in. Finally. Forever.

Whatever happens, life will never be the same again.

Notes

1. Have you ever *heard* a miracle? Duane Miller has written a wonderful book about his entire experience, titled *Out of the Silence*, published by Thomas Nelson Publishers, Nashville, Tennessee (1996). Along with the book comes a copy of the actual tape that recorded Duane's voice as it was healed. This powerful and unique witness is something you will want to share with everyone you know. And if you'd like to contact Duane or schedule him for a talk in your area, contact NuVoice Ministries, P.O. Box 27007, Houston, TX 77227-7007 (Phone: 800-344-0646).

2. Sondra Johnson has had a long and varied career as a writer, editor, and lecturer, perhaps most notably as assistant to renowned author Catherine Marshall, and as executive director of

BreakThrough Ministries, Inc., a national intercessory prayer network; P.O. Box 121, Lincoln, VA 20160 (Phone: 540-338-4131).

3. Angel Network Charities, Inc., is committed to a "hand up, not a handout" and focuses on renting suitable homes within existing neighborhoods for displaced families, particularly for single moms and children. Once housed, the families then work to get back into society's mainstream with job training, schooling, and counseling. The program has about a 96 percent success rate; that is, of all the families accepted for help, only a handful have returned to the streets. For more information or to send a donation, contact Angel Network Charities, Inc., 928 Puuomao Place, Honolulu, HI 96825 (Phone: 808-377-1841).

4. To find out more about Padre Pio's amazing life, contact the Padre Pio Foundation of America, Inc., P.O. Box 2635, Middletown, CT 06457 (Phone: 800-635-4996) or visit its Web site at http://www.padrepio.com

5. Barbara Shleman Ryan is one of the founders of the internationally known Association of Christian Therapists and presently chairs

the Department of Pastoral Care for Trinity College of Graduate Studies in Anaheim, California. She is also president of Beloved Ministry (P.O. Box 9249, Brea, CA 92822), which is devoted to preaching, teaching, and healing.

6. SWAT staff members, along with traveling teams of children, are available to come and train other church staffs. In addition, Pastor Helen Beason has written a pamphlet titled *Children of Purpose—A Generation with Vision* about the development of SWAT, which can be used in any church or organization to help form similar groups. For further information, you can contact her at SWAT Ministries, P.O. Box 105, Litchfield, IL 62056 (Phone: 217-324-6215). The pamphlet can be ordered for $8, which includes postage. Ask about additional training materials.

7. Ken Gaub's latest book, *Rearranging Your Mental Furniture*, is published by Morris Publishing, Kearney, Nebraska (1997). He also has a new video available. For information on Ken Gaub's ministries or speaking engagements or to order the above book, write to him at World Wide Ministries, P.O. Box 1, Yakima, WA 98907 (Fax: 509-575-4732).

Recommended Reading List

Brown, Michael. *The Trumpet of Gabriel*. Milford, Ohio: Faith Publishing Company, 1994.

————. *The Final Hour*. Milford, Ohio: Faith Publishing Company, 1992.

Gellman, Rabbi Marc, and Monsignor Thomas Hartman. *Where Does God Live?* Liguori, Mo.: Triumph Books, 1991. (for children)

Goldwasser, Rabbi Dovid. *It Happened in Heaven*. Jerusalem/New York: Feldheim Publishers, 1995.

Jones, Robin. *Where Was God at 9:02 AM?* Nashville, Tenn.: Thomas Nelson Publishers, 1995. (regarding the Oklahoma City bombing)

McCall, Dr. Kenneth. *Healing the Family Tree*.

London, England: Sheldon Press, 1982. (now available in the United States)

Miller, Duane. *Out of the Silence*. Nashville, Tenn.: Thomas Nelson Publishers, 1996.

O'Connell, Janice. *Meetings with Mary*. New York: Ballantine Books, 1995.

Prather, Paul. *Modern Day Miracles: How Ordinary People Experience Supernatural Acts of God*. Kansas City, KS: Andrews and McMeel, 1996.

Williamson, Martha, and Robin Sheets. *Touched By an Angel*. Grand Rapids, Mich.: Zondervan Publishing House, 1997.

OTHER SOURCES OF INTEREST

Angels on Earth magazine. Guideposts, P.O. Box 39, Seminary Hill Rd., Carmel, NY 10512. Internet site: www.guideposts.org

Miracles are Real video (Questar). Vision Video, P.O. Box 540, Worcester, PA 19490 (800-523-0226). 80 minutes, $19.95

Angels on the Net, e-mail: netangel@netangel.com

Afterword

I am always interested in hearing from readers who would like to share their angel encounters, miracles, answers to prayer, and other heavenly wonders. Please write to me at P.O. Box 127, Prospect Heights, Illinois 60070. Or you can e-mail me at angelwak@mcs.com or visit my Web site at www.mcs.net/~angelwak/home.html.

If I can use your story in my future writing, I will contact you for permission.

—JOAN WESTER ANDERSON

About the Author

Joan Wester Anderson is the bestselling author of *Where Angels Walk, Where Miracles Happen, Where Wonders Prevail, An Angel to Watch Over Me,* and *Angels We Have Heard on High.* Her work, totaling twelve books and over a thousand articles and stories, has been widely published in newspapers and in such magazines as *Reader's Digest, Woman's Day,* and *Modern Bride.* The author has appeared on *Oprah, Good Morning America, NBC Nightly News, Eternal Word Television Network,* and many other national and local shows, and has been featured on several videos dealing with angels and miracles. She and her husband live in a Chicago suburb. They have five grown children and one grandchild.